Great-Grandma Is on Twitter and Other Signs the Rapture Is Near

Great-Grandma Is on Twitter and Other Signs the Rapture Is Near

DIANE LANEY FITZPATRICK

ISBN: 0692544569
ISBN 13: 9780692544563
Library of Congress Control Number: 2015916532
School Night Press, San Francisco, CA

For my mother, Lillian, who constantly told me I was pretty great. And for my mother-in-law, Mary Jo, who still does.

Table of Contents

Introduction

I had been writing funny, for-the-most-part true stories in the guise of a blog for eight years before I decided to take the most popular posts, toss in some of my personal favorites, and turn them into this book. My husband was the first to suggest it.

"You should take all of your blog posts and publish them in an e-book," he said, adding in a murmur, "so the kids have some record of what you've been doing the past few years." He may have read somewhere that you can self-publish *literally in minutes! For FREE!* I knew better but decided to embark on this anyway. Our home renovations were coming to a close, it didn't look like we were going to be moving again anytime soon, and my children were all out of college. I needed a project to justify continuing to call myself a stay-at-home mom. Something short of having more kids, of course.

When I started my blog *Just Humor Me,* I had a child in middle school, another in high school, and a third in college. Sometimes I wrote about them (at great peril; teenagers hate having a writer for a parent in the Internet age); other times I looked back and told stories from my youth or from other eras before blogs were invented. I had a lot of catching up to do. *Just Humor Me* has more than seven hundred posts, all written by me, despite pleading with various out-of-town visitors to guest-blog for me while I mixed up some cocktails.

As you read, you might find me changing my son's diaper on one page and helping him with his college essays on the next. I might be washing my shoulder-length hair with hotel shampoo and a chapter later using my sister's Pureology on what my family now calls my "lobotomy-prep haircut."

So while the stories skip around a bit, know that they're all true. There are exaggerations and misquotes, for sure. But if I say something funny happened, trust me—it happened.

And the funny things continue to happen. I hope to be posting humorous stories long after the Internet has been replaced by the next big thing. Whatever the future holds, I plan to use the writing implement at my disposal to tell you about the time that guy at that place did that thing that one time. I don't expect to run out of fodder for some time to come.

If you like what you read here, you can read more of my stories on *Just Humor Me* at DianeLaneyFitzpatrick.com. Unless you're reading this in the far future, and then have one of the ape masters download it for you.

One

Growing Up in the '60s Is Everything You've Heard Plus Better TV Theme Songs

Once a Baby, Always the Baby in the Family

We just returned from a family visit to my hometown. Which means that the minute our plane touched down in Ohio, I went from being a mature, responsible adult to being a bratty toddler.

I was always the youngest. The youngest of my siblings, which means I always got whatever I wanted. And even when I got married, I was the youngest and newest of the daughters-in-law, which means I always got whatever I wanted, but in a more adult way. When I took more than my share of the shrimp cocktail, no one said anything.

When I was growing up, we would go—not often—to the Red Barn, the 1970s hillbilly version of McDonald's. With five kids and not a lot of money, the rule in our family was that when you went to the Red Barn, you could get either a hamburger and french fries, or you could get a Big Barney, the bigger burger with more layers. I would pout that I wanted both, leaving everyone in my family with an ingrained memory of my nine-year-old voice whining, "But I want a Big Barney *AND* french fries!" I'm sorry to say that I usually got both the Big Barney and fries. Why didn't someone reach into the backseat and smack me but good?

But I was the youngest, so I got my way. I got waited on hand and foot; people gave me things and did things for me because I was the youngest.

Cut to last weekend when my son and daughter and I went to Ohio to visit family. The Red Barn is long gone, having been replaced by The Best Little Hair House in Hubbard or an H&R Block or some such thing, but I was babied all the same.

My mother-in-law sleeps on her couch and gives me her big fluffy queen-sized bed when I visit. She tiptoes around in the morning so I can sleep in. She makes me coffee and practically spoon feeds me casseroles and buttered toast with the crusts cut off. I went to the lake and my brothers- and sisters-in-law cooked me food, took me on boat rides, and brought me drinks. I went empty-handed to my family reunion and mooched off all of my older cousins. And some younger ones too.

I didn't whine about my fast food choices over the course of the weekend, but there was a lot of this coming out of my mouth:

"Does anyone have any Tylenol?"

"Can I wear your perfume?"

"I didn't bring any plates. Can we use yours? Oh, and where's your cooler?"

"Can I borrow your car?"

"I forgot my cell phone charger. Does anyone have a phone I can use to make some calls?"

"Can we get ice cream?"

Honestly, looking back on it, I'm such a baby. Maybe that's why I love going back home so much. It's fun to be little. I'm back in my real adult life now, where I have to make the coffee, cook my own food, and even be the Mom a little bit. There are 358 days until next year's trip back home. This time, I'm going to ask if we can go to the zoo.

Music to Buy Adult Diapers To

There's an old-person radio station here in Florida. No big surprise there, but it's freaking me out a little bit because it reminds me of Stereo 99, this FM station we had in Youngstown in the 1960s and '70s. It was all old people music, mostly instrumental, with some Perry Como and Andy Williams vocals thrown in for variety. Called easy listening, it played on the sound systems of most office buildings and doctors' offices, as well as at Al Tell's Pharmacy, where I worked when I was seventeen.

Every time I hear this Florida radio station I think I'm back at Al Tell's, behind the counter, wearing my white polyester pharmacy helper lab coat and waiting on the following regular customers:

1. The one-hundred-year-old man who is there to buy his wife's diapers and wants help picking them out. I'm a senior in high school, Pops, what do I know?

2. A girl I go to high school with who is poor and married someone even poorer and whose baby is allergic to regular formula, so she has to come in and buy the expensive stuff. Each bottle of this formula costs about as much as my senior picture package. I so want to help her take a case of this formula out of the store without paying for it, but I know that's not in either of our DNAs. She'll put it on her in-store charge account, and a lady from my church will come next week and pay off her bill anonymously with money from the Love Fund. This girl's visit is a rollercoaster of emotions for me.

3. A guy my sister went to school with who is asking me to show him all the different kinds of condoms we have. This was back when condoms were behind a counter and you had to ask a seventeen-year-old pharmacy clerk for them. He drew out his selection for what seemed like forever, trying hard to embarrass me. Not asking him if he wanted the extra small size was one of my major accomplishments in that job and something I probably should have put on my resume.

4. A married guy with four kids who flirts with me and I swear is Munchausening his own elderly mother so he'll have a reason to stop in at the drugstore every single day after work rather than go home to his mom, a frazzled wife, and four wild kids. I saw him with his family at a wedding once and I was like, *Okay, I get it now.*

5. A drug addict who smells so bad I can sniff her coming three aisles away. She brings in this little girl to cough so she can get the terpin hydrate with codeine, a controlled narcotic. She'll sign the narcotics

book (*Name — Endkld Mejjjdpz Address — Motel 6, Sout Side*) and drink the whole bottle on the sidewalk out front before the door has swung shut.

During this parade of the freakers' ball, we're all being serenaded by Stereo 99, playing "Hot Diggity (Dog Ziggity Boom)" and "What Now My Love?"

It was the perfect soundtrack for the place, actually. Some music is just universal in its appeal.

Water, Water Everywhere

My oldest son is home for a few weeks before he leaves for China, where he's going to live for a year or more, teaching English to what could be the cutest little kids on the globe. I'm really excited about his new adventure, but also I'm excited about him being home for a while.

In addition to packing in *Leave It to Beaver* family bonding experiences to last a year, I've promised him some Florida Adventures. They will most likely involve water in various formats, some of them splashing in my face, which is making me slightly anxious.

I'm not the nervous type, but the things I worry about almost all involve water.

Let me start at the beginning, when I was little and my sister Kathy would insist on breaking me away from my overprotective mother to take me to Glen Echo or Yankee Lake or Farmer Jim's to swim. My mom would yell out the back screened door as we packed our beach gear into the car, "Don't drown!"

I read a Dave Barry column in which he said that his mother used to say the same thing to him, except she was kidding. He used that as an example of the cool sense of humor his mom had. I use it as an example of why I close my mouth and plug my nose when I walk by puddles.

While other kids went swimming to have fun, splash around, and play Marco Polo, I just tried to stay among the living. I can safely say that all of my memories involving water are either gruesome, hair raising, or embarrassing. Here they are in roughly chronological order:

- At Glen Echo once, my Tony the Tiger inner tube flipped over with me in it, and I was stuck headfirst in the water, my feet kicking wildly as I tried to right myself. Kathy flipped me over, saving my ever-loving life, and said, "Oh, don't be such a baby. You're fine."
- The first dying body I ever saw was a guy, also at Glen Echo, who dove into the diving area and hit broken glass, came up all bloody, and was laid out on the beach to die the least dignified death, surrounded by a bunch of sunburned kids in bathing caps and Tony the Tiger inner tubes. Note to young self: Don't dive. Ever.
- My grandfather told me he once went into the water before the recommended twenty-minute waiting period after eating, got a stomach cramp, and almost drowned. I believed him, even when each time he told the story, the waiting period increased to twenty-five minutes, a half hour, forty-five minutes...
- My mom signed me up for swim lessons in the basement of a church in Sharon, Pennsylvania, one summer. My friend Diane and I went together, because our moms could carpool. No one seemed to think it weird that a church had a huge swimming pool in its basement. I was so terrified of the swim lessons it's a wonder I didn't turn against all Christianity. To this day the smell of chlorine gives me butterflies. It reminds me of walking from the shower room into the pool area, where I knew the teachers would make fun of me because I wouldn't let go of the side of the pool. No one took pity on me or even tried to teach me how to actually swim. The teachers spent all their time with the kids who already knew how to swim. A year ago, I washed a load of whites with Clorox and the memories came flooding back. I hope those swim teachers are old hags with their own irrational fears by now.
- I spent many summers going to Lake Erie with our neighbors, the fearless Balestrinos, where we gave fate the finger by running along the break wall and swimming way too far into the lake. The Balestrino Family Rule that nothing bad happens to people who take risks proved to be true.

- My high school had swimming as part of gym class, because my town had a community swimming pool conveniently located right next door to the school. Cool, yes? No. Gym class was bad enough with rope climbing, the balance beam, those BO-infused gym uniforms, the trampoline, getting naked in the locker room with the big-boobed girls, modern dance—all of which I sucked at. But add swimming in there and it was enough to get a high school junior to march into the principal's office and say, "Hey, I'm one of the smart girls. Can't I get a freakin' waiver here?" The only perk of having high school swimming was yearbook photos of guys in Speedos. That's the gift that keeps on giving.
- When I first met my husband, I didn't know he was a water/boating person until after I fell in love with him and it was too late to bail. On our third or fourth date, he took me to Lake Milton to walk romantically on the docks in the moonlight and—I am not lying about this, ask him—I was afraid to walk across the dock boards because there was a gap of four or five inches. He married me anyway. Which is cool.

People who knew me growing up think it's ironic that now I have a swimming pool in my backyard and I go to the beach a couple times a week, where I sometimes walk into the ocean up to my neck. And I will even walk on the docks with my husband, where there's a gap of six inches or more.

So there are sure to be water adventures for my China-bound son in the next few weeks. Could someone please yell out "Don't drown!" to us? We may need the encouragement.

It's Time for Michelle Obama Paper Dolls

I've been waiting forty-five years to put paper clothes on a First Lady and, by God, I think this might be my year.

When I was really small, my dad used to go on trips for work and bring us back stuff. One time he brought my sister Pam a Chinese doll that was made of fabric and stuffed solid and covered in layers of silky, satiny colorful Chinese fabrics. I thought he had gone to China.

He was a machinist and actually went to Louisville, Kentucky. (My first clue should have been what he brought my sister Reenie: a scarf with horses and the word KENTUCKY all over it.) At the time, I had no idea what my father did for a living and where he went on those trips. He either fixed machines or was a diplomat in the Foreign Service. Whatever. He always found a gift shop and we got presents.

On one trip, he brought home Jackie Kennedy and Caroline Kennedy paper dolls. They were ginormous, between the size of an American Girl doll and life-size, the better to see the detail in Jackie's shiny black hair.

I was at the start of a thirty-year-long Jackie Kennedy phase and nearly popped a vein when I saw that big black-haired head come out of the bag. Then I saw the giant Caroline come out right after her, and I knew right away what was happening here: Pam was going to get Jackie and I was getting stupid Caroline.

Caroline Kennedy was my age, so the paper doll was Caroline as a five-year-old, with those Peter Pan collars and pleated skirts, white gloves, smocked Easter dress, and a little pedal-pusher sun-top outfit for romping around the Hyannis Port lawn on Sunday afternoons.

Jackie came with a rainbow variety of nubby suits with big buttons and matching pillbox hats, a white sparkly gown, and—if I recall—a horseback riding outfit with a riding crop.

I, of course, acted very happy with my Caroline paper doll. But I added this to my list of reasons why I was jealous of Pam, who also was the only one in our family allowed to grow her hair long.

But now that we're all grown up and I'm old enough to go to Kentucky or China or wherever to buy my own First Family paper dolls, I want to buy a Michelle Obama paper doll.

I'll dress her in the sleeveless dresses with the wide belts, the ruffly inaugural gown, the campaign trail black and beige mix-and-match outfits, and pearls.

Somebody else can have Malia and Sasha with their empire-waisted dresses, bows, matching coats, soccer uniforms, and pedal pushers.

Maybe Pam would want them.

The Hurt Locker, '70s Style

In my high school, on the day of a basketball game, the players would get their lockers decorated. This task fell to a group of girls, loosely organized and without an adviser, whose only requirement was that they not be cheerleaders. The cheerleaders were in early transition to becoming their own sport—although in 1977 they were a long way off from getting their *own* lockers decorated.

Thinking about it now, decorating the lockers should have been assigned to art students. With their creativity and access to supplies, they could have turned locker decorating on its head. But instead it fell to a small group of girls who had no business decorating anything. We may have been the only people who weren't doing anything else on game days.

We were each assigned a player. Mine was Richard, who I'd had a crush on in sixth grade. But I had a crush on almost everyone in sixth grade, including my teacher, so it wasn't awkward at all that by senior year I was taping crepe paper and glitter eagles onto Richard's locker.

Locker decorating was supposed to pump up the players and get them all psyched for the game that night. To do this, we had the following tools in our arsenal:

- Crepe-paper streamers
- Fat letters cut out of construction paper, using fat stencils
- Glitter
- A *Roget's Pocket Thesaurus*

Our school colors were blue and white, so most of the time the crepe-paper streamers and construction paper letters were blue or white, blue and white, blue-white-blue, or some other combination. But by about mid-season, we all got tired of the blue and white, so we ventured into enemy territory and started using the colors of the opposing team. My favorites were the two Catholic schools, Cardinal Mooney, red and gold, and Ursuline, green and gold. The lockers looked great when we played the Catholics.

We'd pick the colors and try to think of a new way to swirl the crepe-paper streamers down or across the locker. Then we'd have to think of a message. The message was always a variation of BEAT the OPPOSING TEAM. And that's where the thesaurus came in. If you look up "beat" in the thesaurus, you'll see there are lots of alliterative ways to win a basketball game.

You could Pound the Panthers. You could Crush the Cardinals. You could do any number of things to the Bulldogs, including the classic Beat. Unfortunately, we also played against the Irish and the Indians, and you could really only Impede them. That sounds like you're encouraging your team to trip the other players or put large pieces of furniture in their path to keep them from scoring. Impeding alone might not even win you the game. I spent more time than I'd like to admit poring over the thesaurus, looking for creative ways to encourage Richard to win a basketball game against various animals and ethnic groups.

Now that I'm older, with twenty-five years of kids' crafts under my belt and a bachelor's degree in a writing-related field, I could totally rock a locker decorator's job. Plus, because I'm not a teenager anymore, I'm not afraid of standing out and having my work be different from the other lockers. Just off the top of my head, without even digging out my old thesaurus, here's one:

White-on-white. Scant sprinkling of white glitter. Paper snowflakes. Letters formed by glued-together plastic icicles. "Ice the Indians."

Two

Get Married, Have Some Kids, and Be Nice Like You Are

Not So Gently Down the Stream

I've never considered myself Super Girl, but after canoeing on the Loxahatchee River last weekend, I can honestly say that I'm fairly useless in the strength department.

Remember that ad for Charles Atlas body building where the skinny guy gets sand kicked in his face by the muscly guy? That's me, but fatter and in a one-piece.

We had two canoes, one for my husband and me, and another for the kids. No matter how hard we paddled—I mean, we were heaving and hoeing like no tomorrow—the kids went gliding on ahead of us.

"How did they get up there so fast?" I said as I looked way upriver and saw them speeding away. "Maybe because they're lighter."

The seven bottles of water, jumbo sunscreen, and canister of bug spray were surely weighing down our boat. Not to mention the extra fifty pounds of body fat we were packing. Meanwhile, the teenagers—dehydrated, bug-bitten, baking in the sun, and skinny—didn't give a rat's ass. They had speed.

And they had more precision and finesse than we did too. We got to a very narrow section of the river, where it was getting potentially alligatory and the water had those floating pieces of green stagnation on it. *Brackish*, my husband said. This is creepy and I'm a little bit scared, I said. (Remember my history with water?)

"Where are they?" I was fending off a big tree branch with my paddle. We kept running into the shoreline, bouncing back and forth like a pinball. "I don't think they came down here. It's too narrow."

Occasionally we would encounter another canoe coming the other way. No, they hadn't seen our kids, but they did see some red spiders that jumped into their boat. I mentally added *Red Spiders* to the list of things I was fearing about this canoe trip—just above Fear #3: Drowning in Brackish Water and right under Fear #1: Having a *Deliverance* Experience.

We never did catch up with the kids. They reached a point of the river where even they didn't feel up to the challenge, so they turned around and found us. They heard me talking to the fish, begging them not to jump into our boat, and they paddled right past us.

"But these fish, they are jumping so high!" I whined. "They could have spiders on them. Or *brack*."

As the kids' canoe glided past us, I noticed their paddles were moving in perfect synchronization. They looked like a small crew team out of uniform. That was the problem: My husband and I were not working together. I was paddling with every ounce of strength in my body and he . . . he . . . what was he doing back there anyway?

"You're paddling, aren't you?" I was afraid to turn around, because every time I moved the canoe tipped a little bit, putting me closer to Fear #3.

"Yeah, sure. I'm paddling," he said.

I could have sworn I heard a beer can being popped.

Which Line Is the Drum One?

I may be the worst band mom in recent history.

I have a daughter in band but I don't exactly fit the profile.

I haven't yet volunteered for any really big meaningful jobs. Like Band Camp Snack Bringer. Or Sausage & Trinket Sale Coordinator. I helped supervise at a car wash once. But that was only because the mom who was really in charge got a little bit overwhelmed, the kids were out of control, and she got soap in her mouth. Close to tears, she folded up her chair, threw her sponges in her trunk, and drove away. I didn't know we were allowed to do that. I stepped in and took over, gathering the soaking-wet teenagers together and pleading with them not to be a-holes for just, like, a thirty-minute stretch. That didn't win me any points with the Band Booster upper management.

I don't take the time to learn anything about the music. I really only watch my own kid, so when the other parents say things like, "Drum line has to learn the 3/4 4/4 alternating time in Section 3 by Tuesday," I chime in with "Heck yeah!" just to show them I'm listening. I'm not even sure I know which line the drum one is.

And while I ordered the big salad-plate-sized photo pin of my daughter in her band uniform, I have never worn it. It doesn't fit in my jewelry box, and it's not really jewelry anyway, is it? It covers my entire chest. I think I could wear it as a top. I stashed it in a box with my AARP invitation under the label "Things I Should Deal with But They're Bad for My Self-Esteem."

It's not that I'm incapable of handling stage mother duties. I can put together a spaghetti dinner at my house for eighty cross-country team members without too much spillage. I can take pictures in focus of high schoolers running really fast and kicking a ball. I can coordinate, delegate, supervise, chair, and co-chair the living daylights out of anything related to school, sports, or other organized groups.

The problem is that I wasn't in band when I was in high school, so I just don't get it. I don't fit in with the other band moms, because they are all former French horn players or flautists who still remember what their moms did for them. I was in choir, and we didn't have moms.

I've tried to change my ways. I even lent a hand with uniforms once. The band was at a highway rest stop, and suddenly big garment racks were wheeled out of a truck and the kids all scrambled for their uniforms. I jumped in and started calling out names, snapping spats, and putting feathers in caps. When the whirling dervish was over and the uniformed kids sped away on buses, I was standing in the parking lot with one black sock, a white glove, and a trumpet. "This can't be good," I said, and stuffed them into one of the snack coolers.

Last year I showed up at band camp to watch, thinking that was pretty band mom-ish of me. There were twenty-five or thirty other parents there, in the middle of the day, lined up on folding chairs, with Band-aids and smelling salts at the ready, all intently watching the practice. Some of them were on cell phones telling someone I can only guess was the other parent that Travis was 1/16th of a beat off at the end of Part One.

"He'll be practicing that at home tonight," the mom said menacingly. I watched for a while, saw that it was pretty much a bunch of hot, sweaty teenagers standing with their hands together in fists up to their mouths, elbows out, performing endurance exercises, while a couple of the seniors spray-painted the asphalt. Other than the weaklings who were crumpled to the ground, not much was happening. I snapped a few pictures and went home.

This year could be better. I've already signed up to help at band camp for two days, I'm bringing a couple cases of Gatorade one day, and I put my name on some sign-up sheets for something or another. I even got the health form notarized.

I think I might be becoming a real band mom. Choir moms, watch and learn.

Serious Parenting, Seriously

As you may know, my serious writing job is doing parenting articles for an online content provider. And by serious writing job I don't mean serious job, I mean serious writing. Any job that you can do from your house while on hold with Apple tech support and wearing nothing from the waist down cannot be considered serious.

But to write about parenting, I have to read a lot about parenting. I've broken my old rule of Don't Ever Read a Self-Help Book, and I've read lots of self-help books on parenting troubled teens (Message: Listen to them with a sympathetic tilted head and furrowed brow and then do what you would have done anyway), parenting Terrible Twos (Message: Drink heavily and hang on until Thorazine Threes), parenting step-kids (Message: You really *aren't* the boss of them, as it turns out), and everything in between.

It seems that every parent on earth is a better parent than me, except for the people on *Supernanny*, who are way, way worse than me. Which is why I love that show more than some of my extended family. I'd take a bullet for Jo just so she could continue to go into people's homes and tell them what a lousy job they're doing as parents. I'm going to admit some things here so prepare yourselves; what you're about to read may shock you, particularly the better parents among you.

I never used 1-2-3 Magic or any other child discipline method that earned the Good Housekeeping Seal of Approval.

I shocked my play group when they were gossiping about a Brownie Scout mom who "didn't even know what 1-2-3 Magic is!"

"What's 1-2-3 Magic?" I asked. They spit out their daiquiris, and somebody choked on a maraschino cherry.

"You don't use 1-2-3 Magic? Oh my God!" The six of them stared at me. Someone said snippily, "I don't know how you could have had three kids and survived up to this point without using 1-2-3 Magic."

Eventually, after a few more drinks, they explained to me that 1-2-3 Magic is *only* the most effective form of child discipline in the history of childrearing. It has something to do with counting to three, which, when I was growing up, wasn't a parenting method but just what some of the more considerate dads did before taking off their belts and beating the crap out of their kids.

After listening to the explanation, I asked, "Well, what if you count to three and they still won't do what you asked them to do?" I apparently just didn't get it. I think I needed to read the book. But that might explain why I don't use common everyday parenting methods. I'm afraid they won't work and then I'll really be up a creek. Which brings me to my second thing:

I never put my kids in time-out.

I know, Jo is probably choking on her own maraschino cherry right now, just thinking about that. But it's true. I don't know whether it's because my kids were really not that bad or I was just afraid they would look at the stool in the corner and say, "Poop on that, I'm outta here." I just couldn't see myself in a physical battle with my kids, even during the short period of time when I was taller than them.

I lied for them.

I am the world's worst liar, but if they didn't want to go to Kassy's house to play with the Madame Alexander dolls in the boxes, I became an excellent liar. I would grab the phone out of their hands and say, "Yeah, hey, Kass, the kids can't come over today because I'm having ovarian surgery at two." She was little; she didn't know surgeries aren't scheduled for the afternoons.

There are times to teach your kids the big life lessons about truth and facing up to responsibilities—facing the hard stuff head-on—and there are times you just have to lie for them. I always told my kids I would be their excuse, their front man, the one-who-lies-to-get-them-out-of-a-jam. To this day there are kids all over the country who think I was the strictest mom and that my kids could never come over to their houses because of me and my surgeries.

I'm sure, according to some parenting expert, that this makes me a Hovering Helicopter Parent or a Default Parent, or just a Lazy Scared Liar. I don't care. Please don't tell the readers of my serious parenting articles.

School Supply Madness

My husband and I were wandering around Home Depot the other day (when you're married twenty-five years and living the dream, this can happen more often than you would think), and we were discussing school starting in about two weeks. "You're going to have to get school supplies," he said, and I did not pop a vein.

This must be what everyone talks about when you're entering Pre-Empty Nest and have only one kid at home; your life goes from bad porn movie without the sex to a made-for-TV movie you might watch all the way through if there aren't any *Law & Order* reruns on. It's God's way of easing you slowly back into real life without the shock.

With only one child in school and that school being high school, I no longer have to call in a bomb threat to Staples to get all the supplies my kids need by the first day of school. I'm not sure why, but this year getting school supplies is one of the mellower items on my list of things to do by August 18.

It wasn't always like this. When I had three kids in different schools, the school supply lists were like my Koran. I prayed they would come to me early, in a dream, and give me the advantage I needed to kick the other parents' asses in the First Day of School Competition and Teacher Brown Nose Contest.

Teachers and the other schooly people held the school supply list just above our reach and used it as their last weapon before we retaliated by sending our kids to them to take care of for free every weekday for nine months.

When my oldest son was in high school, the school staffers handed us parents the supply list at orientation, always held the night before the first day of school. Orientation was the thing where they made all the kids and parents squeeze into the auditorium at the same time and get vital information about school that they couldn't dispense any other way. It wasn't available before that day, it couldn't be put on a website or posted on a large bulletin board outside the school building, and it couldn't be mailed to the parents ahead of time. You had to show up at orientation to get everything you needed to know. Parents were known to camp out in the parking lot just to get a parking spot, then make a mad dash out of there at the end so they could get to Staples before everyone else.

The teachers, I swear, would just sit back and wallow in the knowledge that grownups were doing their bidding and even blocking fire lanes at the shopping plaza to get the rare *Two-inch Binder With Pocket in Front Cover Only, Four (4) Rings, Forest Green ONLY* before they ran out.

"I have a *master's degree*," I heard one mom telling the Staples store manager, her voice cracking, the list shaking in her hands. It just didn't seem fair that we could be such good parents and still have to send our kids to school missing required items.

There were elementary school years when, in an unexplained attempt to corner the Tiger Mom market, Walmart would somehow get a hold of black market school supply lists and put them in a cardboard holder at the front of the store. The idea was to find your school, get the list, and buy your stuff ahead of time. The only problem was that they were lists from previous years or they were just plain fake (clue: there is no such thing as a No. 8 pencil), or the slot for our school was empty. It was just a big tease, another cruel trick that made me wonder if the Walmart smiley face wasn't actually smirking.

By the time we did get the school supply list, that section of the store was a mess—nothing in the right places, rulers and protractors strewn all over the floor, and aisles jammed with people frantically grabbing at things. And there was always that clueless dad who actually tried to negotiate a shopping cart in there. Chances of us getting the things on the list before a Who-concert-like trampling incident occurred was slim to none.

The teacher would often require each child to bring in a box of Kleenex, hand sanitizer, diaper wipes, or antibacterial soap to donate to the classroom—items that made me wonder if I was smart to even send my child to public school, with all that communal snot, sweat, and spit spraying around. But then I would look at my cart full of composition notebooks, color-coded folders, $200 Texas Instrument calculators, and Trapper Keepers and think, *Hell, I don't care what they pick up; I got my hands on this crap and it's going into their backpacks and into a school building.*

Homeschool parents, don't tell me you DIY your kids' education because they are light-years ahead of their peers in math and science and your third grader just scored a 1500 on his SAT. You just can't handle the school supplies, can you? You saw the size of the list one year and turned to your husband and said, "You know, dear, I'm thinking I could probably teach the kids better myself." And with the money you save on school supplies, you could hire Yo-Yo Ma to come in and teach them music.

Why I Seem Weird: A Mother's Day Letter to My Kids
Dear kids,

Happy Mother's Day! To me! I couldn't have gotten here without you. Thank you for all of your Mother's Day gifts over the past twenty-three years, all the kisses and hugs, handmade pictures of your handprints, flowers, and funny cards with other people's heads Photoshopped into pictures with me. I appreciate everything you've ever given me but will not stop requesting to go to Waffle House for breakfast until I finally get my wish.

I'd like to take this opportunity to explain why I've done some of the stupid things I've done since you were born. Parenting is the weirdest job in the world. You can't even imagine it. You'll think you know yourself and your decision-making abilities, and then you'll have kids and find yourself allowing and forbidding things that make sense to no one but you. Trust me, and remember this letter when you're thirty-five and you allow your ten-year-old to go to Europe with the neighbors who you suspect are going there to score drugs, but you won't let him cross the street without holding your hand. It may not make sense now, but when you're a parent it will seem perfectly normal.

Parenting is basically a series of decisions. Starting with breast or bottle, cloth or disposable, pacifier or listen to a screaming baby go through withdrawal, and continuing into public school or private, soccer or cheerleading, the shirt she wants to wear or the shirt you want her to wear, yes you can go over to Jessie's house or no Jessie's parents have guns and they smoke. Parenting is just decision after decision. There are no patterns. And frankly we have no idea what we're doing.

There is no test you have to pass to be a parent. No one asks you any questions on your way out of the hospital with your newborn, other than "did you take any supplies home in your suitcase?" And even if there were questions and you answered incorrectly, you would still be allowed to take your baby home and raise it however you wanted.

There is no 1-800 number you can call with your questions. You have to wait until you screw up and do something wrong, and then you're allowed to call the police or poison control, where you'll get a lecture on how not to do that ever again. *Yeah, well, I know that now. Where were you before this happened?*

We're all just winging it, letting you do some things and forbidding you from doing other things. *Yes, no, no, yes, no, yes, yes, no, we'll see, are you kidding? Absolutely not.* Day in and day out.

Remember the time I let Mike ride in the trunk of the minivan, curled up in a ball for an entire week when we had company and wanted to fit everyone into the same vehicle? And then I wouldn't let him go in the water at the beach, for fear he'd drown or get eaten by sharks. Dry as a bone and alive, I stuffed him into the trunk for the death-defying ride home.

I let you eat lunchmeat that had warning labels on it, but then I cut it up into really small pieces so you wouldn't choke.

Jack, I let you go to the top of some of the tallest structures in the country, in some of the most rickety elevators in the world, but I wouldn't let you play football.

Mike, when you send me photos of you in China, I can look at the ones where you're walking through an opium den, posed next to people with strange satanic tattoos, eating things with eyeballs and antennae, and standing in your apartment, which I notice has no smoke alarms or carbon monoxide detectors, and I'll be just fine. However, when I look at the photo of you standing on top of a cliff near Dalian I will silently scream, "YOU'RE TOO CLOSE TO THE EDGE! GET HOME RIGHT NOW!"

The things we fear for you are irrational. The things we don't fear for you and let you do with a clear conscience don't make any sense either.

I know you're all grown up now, and I'm fine with most of the adventurous stuff you do, but I still won't let you go to the Grand Canyon unless you're on a leash.

You'll understand when you have kids of your own.

Now one of you, climb up on that broken ladder and get me that box of old pictures off the top shelf of the garage. I need to reminisce and celebrate that my excellent parenting has kept you alive and safe thus far.

Congratulations, Said the Airhorn

I'm not going to say one single snarky thing about my daughter's graduation ceremony this morning. Even though the diploma is sitting on my kitchen counter right now, I still fear her guidance counselor's powers. It still might not be safe to diss the high school, because they could reach out from the alumna-grave and hurt our family.

So, yes, the commencement ceremony—for which we had to leave the house at 5:45 a.m., fistfight for a parking spot, beg the $35-diploma-plaque hawkers to please please leave us alone if you have an ounce of mercy in your commission-riddled soul—was lovely.

It was just lovely.

My daughter kept her cell phone tucked in her bra. Wait. Did I just say that? No, she didn't. She didn't break a single rule of the graduation ceremony. She did everything right and there are no problems here, officers.

The rules were announced at the onset of the ceremony, in the cheerful-yet-authoritative voice of the principal. They were also flashed up on the big screen and drilled into the graduates' brains at rehearsal. I believe they were told that if their parents broke any of the rules, their final transcripts would be shredded and 100 points would be subtracted from their SAT scores.

PLEASE STAY IN YOUR SEATS DURING THE CEREMONY AND DO NOT GET OUT OF YOUR SEATS TO TAKE PHOTOGRAPHS

NO AIRHORNS

PLEASE KEEP YOUR APPLAUSE TO A MINIMUM SO EVERYONE CAN HEAR THE GRADUATES' NAMES

ABSOLUTELY NO AIRHORNS

AT THE CONCLUSION OF THE CEREMONY PLEASE WAIT UNTIL THE GRADUATES HAVE FILED OUT AND THEN EXIT BY THE SIDE DOOR AND WAIT FOR YOUR GRADUATE IN THE REAR OF THE BUILDING

IF YOU BLOW AN AIRHORN WE WILL HURT YOU

NO FOOD OR DRINK IN THE CONVENTION CENTER

IF WE HEAR EVEN ONE SQUEAK FROM AN AIRHORN PEOPLE WILL DIE AND WE'RE NOT KIDDING

GRADUATES PLEASE DO NOT THROW YOUR HATS OR MAKE ANY DISRUPTIVE NOISES DURING THE CEREMONY

THE MINUTE WE HEAR AN AIRHORN WE WILL TAKE THE SALUTATORIAN AND CLASS HISTORIAN AND YOU WILL NEVER SEE THEM AGAIN. WE KNOW HOW TO GET TO THE EVERGLADES, AND BELIEVE YOU ME THERE WILL BE NO TRACE OF THESE TWO HIGH ACHIEVERS

Rumor has it that back in the late '90s when airhorns were cheap and easy to conceal, one of the soon-to-be-retired English IV teachers lost three of her senses because of an enthusiastic parent.

Our high school is huge. There were 713 people in my daughter's graduating class. Quite a few towns in Pennsylvania have a population of less than that, towns with their own post office and a couple of traffic lights. So even though almost 90 percent of the graduates are going to college after today, some are just proud as peacocks that they got through high school.

My daughter is not one of those students. If she was such a slacker that graduating from high school was something to blow an airhorn about, I would have to smack her upside the head, possibly with the butt of said airhorn.

"We're so proud of you!" parents tell their children at this milestone. We don't really do that.

"Good job with that GPA," we tell her.

"Yeah, whatever," she responds.

I couldn't find a card that properly expressed our pride at her accomplishments but was not overly gushy. So our gift to her was that we did not get out of our seats during the ceremony, we did not use flash photography (that wasn't a rule, but we were just being safe), and we did not bring our coffee into the convention center.

And we left the airhorns in the car. For later. Much later, when it's safe.

Hi Mom, I'm Home

It's mid-May, and for many of us it's the time when our college kids come home for summer break. Check back with me in late May to see if I'm still alive or if I've been strangled by a dirty sock.

My son arrives home from Phoenix tonight. No, not University of Phoenix online college. If he was getting a degree by sitting at the computer all day, I'd know it. I think. He goes to Arizona State, and he's only been home twice since he started there last August. Whoever said the middle child gets lost in the shuffle didn't know our family. I miss him every day. It could be because he's very funny and personable and fun to be around. He's tall, so he can reach things for me that no one else can. And he knows lots of movie trivia and sports stats, so he's handy to have around at parties and discussions.

The child who goes away to college and then returns home for the summer is in a quandary. He's been living on his own, without his mom telling him to set his alarm clock, don't go to sleep with the computer on, don't put metal in the microwave, and pick his clothes up off the floor. He lived through it all without doing any of those things. He knows the truth now: that you actually *won't* die from eating Hot Pockets and Totino's Pizza Rolls for three meals a day for six weeks, and that you can skip Mass and not get struck by lightning.

And now suddenly he's home again and there's Mom, getting all up in his grill with her demands and questions and requests to get things off the high shelves and using phrases like *getting all up in his grill.* Will she never shut up? No, apparently she will not.

When kids go off to college, the parenting builds up. Every day we normally would say "Are you flossing?" but we can't, it doesn't just dissipate and go off into space. It builds up. Go a few months in between visits home and you're likely to be bombarded at the airport with a list of questions, advice, Confucius sayings, and Bible verses.

"Choose a job you love and you will never have to work a day in your life," many moms say to their children as they're unpacking. "Also, what deodorant are you using these days? Are you always going to wear your hair like that now?"

It will take three-quarters of the summer for me and my son to get our mom-kid groove back, and then we'll go on a family vacation, which will require another adaptation—to the Stockholm syndrome of being imprisoned in a foreign country unnaturally close to relatives. And before we know it, it'll be time for him to go back to school.

Ah cripes, he's not even home yet and I've mentally got him packed to leave. I really am looking forward to him being home. I hope he can *not* kill me long enough for me to miss him when he leaves again.

My Clean-Upmanship

I spent the first four days home after taking my kids to college cleaning out their rooms, not exactly what was promised in the "Now It's Time for You!" chapter of the empty nester's manual.

But I was glad to do it. Extremely glad to do it.

I had given up on my daughter's room from the time we started talking about her going away to college—a full twelve months before she would move out. I had constantly nagged her to pick the clothes up off the floor so I could vacuum it. I fretted about the stains on her carpet that wouldn't come out. I threatened to do a total reorg of her room, and I even went so far as to buy some cute closet organizers. She was not at all interested.

One day she said, "Why don't you just wait until I leave for college and then you can do whatever you want with my room." * scribble scribble scrabble scratch * I etched those words into my brain for later.

For the next year I didn't fuss about her room. When we had company I closed her bedroom door and told people my husband was sterile and we were childless.

So when I returned home from moving her and her brother into their college school-year temporary residences, I didn't waste any time getting my hands on those rooms.

And, oh, the stuff I found.

It was like a TV show, half *Hoarders* and half *Let's Make a Deal*. What's that you say, Monty? Has anyone got an instruction manual for a cell phone that no one owns anymore? Why, I've got seven of them right here!

Some more things I found in my kids' rooms during the big cleanup:

• Clothes with the price tags still on them. These are clothes that some-one *had* to have right then. Clothes that were not on sale. Clothes that I had my doubts would ever be worn.

- A dead frog.
- A check for $200, uncashed, dated two years ago.
- Ten years of *Sports Illustrated* magazines in a crate intended to hold two years' worth of a magazine I had no idea would be renewed so many times. Who knew there would be so much to say about sports? Remember, *SI* comes out every week pretty much, so with special issues, the swimsuit issue (which is as big as the JCPenney catalog; yeah, and is that necessary? No, it's not), anniversary extras, and the months that our subscriptions overlapped and we got two of each issue, we're talking about some six hundred magazines. Some were worth keeping, because a lot has happened in sports since 2002. When my son started getting this magazine, LeBron James hadn't yet signed with the Cavs the first time, Lance Armstrong had only won four Tours de France, Brett Favre looked like he was fourteen, and nobody in baseball was taking steroids.
- Drumsticks. No one in our house ever played the drums. Ever.
- Lots of movie stubs, theater and concert programs, receipts, birthday cards, and boarding passes that I couldn't decide were junk or keepsake memorabilia. No one is as sentimental as me, but it's possible they wanted to remember that trip to Dunkin' Donuts in February 2009 for some reason.
- A mouth guard that I spent several hundred dollars on, which was not covered under insurance but was oh so necessary. Clean as a whistle. Obviously never saw the inside of a mouth.
- A bunch of *my* stuff. Books that I swore I owned but could never find, the good scissors, all the Sharpies in the fun colors, and a couple of DVDs *they* bought *me* for Christmas. I'm starting to wonder if they want me to have anything nice at all.

I read an article once in which a psychologist tried to explain why teenagers have messy rooms. One of the reasons was "futility." What? Futility? *It's just going to get messy again, so why bother cleaning it when my time is better spent watching TV and eating Pringles? And then I'll toss the empty can onto the pile of clothes I just brought home from H&M, which are now mixed in with the clothes to give to Goodwill. And then I'll ponder the meaning of life.* I'm sorry, but teen-agers are not allowed to use "futility" for a reason not to do something their mother wants them to do. Suddenly they're now philosophers?

When they come home for the first break, there better be no complaints about what I've done in their rooms. I got your futility, right here.

Three

WHAT'S GREAT ABOUT GETTING OLDER? LET ME COUNT THE WAYS. WHAT'S ZERO PLUS NEGATIVE ONE?

Eight Great Things About Being Old

Old people have the world by the tail. And they're swinging it around like a crazy, stoned teenager who knows he's going to juvy and doesn't care.

I've decided that old people can see and hear just fine. Their reflexes are better than the average twenty-five-year-old, and the only thing better than their short-term memory is their racecar driving skills. They're faking it and getting away with it.

I can't wait until I'm old now.

1. I can back up my big Cadillac from parking spots in busy commercial lots without looking behind me to see if anyone's coming. I won't need a rearview mirror at all. In fact, I'm going to have the rear and side view mirrors removed from my silver Lincoln. I'll be free to just hit the gas and go. Driving will no longer require any neck strain.

2. I can pretend not to hear what I don't want to hear, pretend not to understand what I don't agree with, pretend not to see what I can't stomach, and pretend I don't understand why I can't use eight coupons at Bed Bath & Beyond for six items, until the frustrated cashier just takes $10 off my bill.

3. I can wear elastic-waist pants and pull them up so high they double as a support bra without winning Dowdiest Female at my class reunion.

4. I can take what my kids have been dishing out to me since I turned forty, mix it up a little bit, and serve it right back to them. My kids claim they tell me things and that I "must've forgotten." You forget a couple things over the years, like to get them braces and a scoliosis check, and they never let you forget it. I know they're lying when they say they already told me "four times" that they need a note for school, that Brian needs a ride to practice, and that their wrist is still swollen and is surely broken. Yeah, yeah, yeah. I think I would have remembered if they actually told me the same thing four times. But that's fine, because two can play at that game. When I'm old, I'm going to not only forget all that, but I'm going to "forget" the stuff I do remember hearing. They'll be lucky to get birthday presents.

5. I can turn the TV up so loud I drown out my husband's music and the dog's sickening digestive tract noises.

6. I can talk super loud on my cell phone without embarrassing myself and those with me. Recently, I was at a local college picking up my daughter from her bassoon lesson and was talking to my husband on the phone as I walked into the building, waited for the elevator, got in the elevator, and rode it up to the fourth floor. When the elevator door opened, I stood face to face with my daughter, who was shooting flames out of her eyes at me. "Everyone up here could hear your whole conversation from downstairs, all the way up the elevator!" she hissed.

   "SORRY!" I'm going to shout. "I'M HARD OF HEARING. AND I'M OLD. SO SHOVE OFF!"

7. I can use quaint, homespun words and phrases that make me look like a moron right now. Folksy things like "inkling" and "that's just peachy" and "smidgen" and "thongs."

8. I can eat lunch at ten in the morning, dinner at two, and have breakfast for the next day before I go to bed at night. And if anyone says anything disparaging about that, I can just say, "WHAT????"

Where Are My Reading Glasses?

No, really, that's not just a title, I really want to know. Do you know where they are? Because I can't find a single pair of them.

For about the tenth time since I turned forty, I had a spontaneous disappearance of all reading glasses in my house and car.

It's the freakiest thing. Perhaps you're old too and this has happened to you. You have reading glasses of all sizes, shapes, and colors sprinkled all over the house, just waiting to be picked up when you find you can't read a recipe, or see which buttons to press on the house alarm to ward off an embarrassing visit from the police, or read a text from your daughter that she needs $5 for a gym locker. (Squinting without glasses, you might think she heads SS for a gum hooker.) You purposefully put a pair of glasses in your car glove box, another in your purse, one on the nightstand, one in the kitchen drawer, one at the computer. The rest you flung like confetti while standing in the center of the house, hoping that some would land in the couch cushions, which is a perfect place to find a pair of glasses in a pinch.

One day you leave a pair of them on a restaurant table, but, hey, no problem. You've got ninety-seven other pairs that you got in your Christmas stocking or your mother-in-law picked up for you at Marc's for ninety-nine cents. They're everywhere, right? Wrong.

You go home and the reading glasses are all AWOL. Even the Extreme Emergency Only pair, the big gold aviator glasses your son found on the high school track one day and brought home to you like a well-trained bag lady's kid. If reading glasses could drink Kool-Aid and commit mass suicide at the same time, they would and they did, I think, in my house a number of times, including this past week.

Being in your fifties and not having a pair of reading glasses is the pits. You might as well be blind as a bat. And I don't know about you, but I can't hear well or think reasonably when I can't see.

Reading glasses and the need for them doesn't make any sense. When I was forty-eight, my eye doctor told me, "You're going to need glasses soon."

"Oh, honey, please. I've had glasses since the second grade and contact lenses since ninth," I told him, trying to sound superior and mature while sitting behind the Batman mask eye-looker-inner thingy.

"No, I mean you're going to need reading glasses for on top of your contact lenses. To read," he said.

I don't understand how a person can be nearsighted and farsighted at the same time. I don't understand why every actor who plays the president has little half-moon reading glasses. I don't understand what happened to all of mine that I paid dozens of dollars for and they just disappeared.

I do understand that not being able to find my glasses and making one of my offspring hold a restaurant menu across the room, tilted up toward the light, officially makes me my mother.

I Too Feel Bad About My Neck

I hope I'm not plagiarizing Nora Ephron, but I'm a firm believer that mimicry is the most adorable form of flattery, and I need all the help I can get. Especially in the neck area.

I'm long overdue for night creams and wrinkle reducers and youth serums and other products I think are amazing when I see the infomercials, but then hate like poison when I have to go on a payment plan to afford them. So when I walked into Sephora yesterday and stage-whispered to the first black-lab-coated saleswoman who walked up to me, "I need something for this," and grabbed my gobbler and stretched it out, I realized the whole scene should have happened about five years ago.

But it didn't. It happened yesterday, and I'm not going to agonize over that. I'm slow to catch up to my actual age. My brain and heart seem to be about five to ten years behind my body and its slow, steady decay. There are several reasons for this.

One, I'm immature. Two, I hate the time and effort it takes to try to look good. It just doesn't seem worth it. I feel like I'm too smart to spend more than a few minutes and a few cents per day on my looks. I mean, really, I only just a few years ago started using product in my hair. Six months before that I didn't even know what *product* meant.

And third—don't laugh—when I was a young girl, I fantasized about being a middle-aged housewife. While other girls were imagining a future as an actress or Speaker of the House or even shift supervisor at the hospital, I was leafing through the JCPenney catalog and fantasizing that I was in my forties and had a bunch of kids, a handsome husband, and a three-bedroom ranch with a finished basement. And then I would pretend the whole family was going out to a picnic or a wedding or some event, and I would pick out all our outfits. I would plan my own look from the models, who were conveniently all middle-aged housewife types. I was classy and sensible with a frosted flip hairdo and understated makeup, and I possessed a beauty so deep that all the peach-and-mauve plaid polyester couldn't hide it.

I had lots of other fantasies, some that had me accomplishing a lot more than matching the purse and shoes I wore to the neighborhood Fourth of July gathering, but the most prominent vision of my future was that of a gracefully aging woman.

So when the crow's feet, mousy hair, and saggy jaw started to appear in my real life, I wasn't all that freaked out. Botox and plastic surgery were not an option. (Have you seen Melanie Griffith lately?) I had to muster up some energy even to deal with it at all. I'm inexplicably and unapologetically comfortable looking my age. So at first I just dimmed the lights and bought a Photoshop package. It wasn't until I saw my neck in a selfie that I thought, *Oh hell. It's time to hit Sephora.*

The black-coated saleswoman led me to the way-back of the store, where they keep the non-makeup makeup, and introduced me to Jeff, a skin care expert. I was relieved he wasn't seventeen, and as far as I could tell he didn't even color his hair, let alone sport any other enhancements that are so popular with Sephora employees. To tell the truth, Jeff looked a little out of place. He and I were the only ones not wearing three shades of eye shadow.

I repeated my neck problem and he started nodding his head halfway through my declaration.

"I know exactly what you mean," he said. "I'm fifty-seven." Oh thank God. He walked directly over to a shelf and picked up two DERMAdoctor products and told me that's what I needed. Then he told me how much it was going to cost me. "Is that more than you wanted to spend?"

"Nobody *wants* to spend $156 to make one notecard-sized patch of skin look better," I said. "Do you sell turtlenecks? 'Cause you should." When Sephora opens a clothing line in the way-way-back of the store, remember, I thought of it first.

High Heels Are a Shoe-In

About two weeks ago I had a big fancy gala to go to.

Upon realizing that I was required to wear a floor-length gown, I called my daughter and asked if she'd go dress shopping with me. Not so much because she's young and cute and hip and wouldn't let me look too bad, but more because she's not afraid to hurt my feelings and will tell me if I look like I'm wearing a Halloween costume. Remember, the Wicked Witch of the West wore an evening gown every time she left the haunted castle.

"Yes, of course I'll come with you," she said.

"I'm not sure I can pull off a gown," I whined. I had tried on a few three years ago at a gown-optional fundraiser and ended up going with a short sequined dress instead because, well, I was convinced I couldn't pull off a gown.

"Of course you can," my daughter assured me. "But you're going to have to wear really high sparkly shoes."

Oh. So *that's* where I went wrong before. I went barefoot in the dressing room—I mean, my legs and feet weren't even visible—but I realize now the shoes you wear all the way down there will affect how you look in a dress from the waist up.

At my age, I probably shouldn't even consider wearing high-heeled sparkly shoes. But here's a little-known fact about getting older: We all know the effect of discomfort on your body rises as you age. But so does your ability to tough it out. And I'm at the point where my quest for being comfortable when out in public is a pipe dream. Unless I'm wearing a flannel nightgown and a cloth diaper, and reclining on a stretcher, there's going to be some level of irritating scratchiness, something is going to be too tight, some internal organ will be squeezed, and various patches of skin will be rubbed by leather, stiff fabric, plastic, or metal. I can't even wear some pierced earrings comfortably because the wires are too thick for my ears.

You know how doctors tell old people, "You have to learn to live with the pain"? They're preaching to the choir. I live with low-level pain every time I get dressed in the morning.

The good news is that you get used to it over time. And at that point, you're full circle, back to wearing high-heeled sparkly shoes. Because if you're not going to be comfortable in Crocs, you may as well go whole hog.

And that's just what I did for this gala. Not only did I buy the gold glitter heels, I bought a pair in silver for next time. I bought a gown that had more metal in it than fabric. You've heard of the corset part of a dress having "boning"? My dress had a full skeleton sewn in it. Which was fine until I sat down. Or tried to breathe. Or stepped out of the taxi. I felt like someone had slipped a science lab skeleton inside my dress and it was fighting to get out.

But it was all good, because I'm one tough middle-aged broad. I saw two women at the gala carrying shoe bags. They wore flats until they were sitting down, and then they popped on their fancy heels for the sitting parts. One of them had flats that exactly matched her heels. Well played, gala lady. Well played.

Me? I'm not ready for the flats and shoe bag route just yet. The shoe bag handle would rub the spot on my arm that my watch has chafed raw.

Four

If We're Living in the Future, Why Don't I Have a Rosie the Robot to Clean for Me?

You Can Call Us Back in a Campbell and Go

Answering machine messages are more entertaining to me right now than anything on TV. The Kardashians can't hold a candle to what's coming in on my regular home phone.

We went to an art museum in Fort Lauderdale not long ago and I became mesmerized by a piece called Karaoke Wrong Number, which was a small TV screen mounted to the wall with a woman mouthing answering machine messages left by strangers calling her at home at the wrong number. I've since found out that this work, by artist Rachel Perry Welty, is somewhat well known and has been to Boston and New York and beyond. While all the other art patrons, including my family, were checking out the regular art, I sat and watched Karaoke Wrong Number all the way through. Twice.

I am equally mesmerized by my Google voice mail transcriptions. Thanks to my husband and his need to out-tech everyone else on the block, we have a new phone system that's on par with the security surveillance at the National Archives. In its quest to be a multimedia extravaganza, our phone sends email messages to my iPhone when I get a voice mail. So while I'm in line at Starbucks, I can see what calls I'm missing right at that moment.

That's all great, except the message transcriber must be in the robot remedial class. He doesn't quite get it right. My mother-in-law and I were at a three-day music event in Tampa, and during a break we read some of my messages and decided I needed to share them. If only to explain why we laughed through an entire jazz set.

Here are four messages I received while in Tampa, lifted directly from the emails I received:

> *"Just just before but I was calling. Bob and I, my mom 02 and she was gonna see what the weather was like, and I'm sure it's 7580. You know it's been zero my dear, Yes, this is a call from Hell, then, thank you from. My with the golf when I get golfing from a golf thing from. Yeah, I could give me one way ticket to gear up so you can call us back in a Campbell and go. Bryce bye bye."*

That message was from my brother-in-law Bob, who actually does like to golf, but maybe not as much as this message suggests. And the weather in Florida that day was not 7,580 degrees, I don't care what anyone says. I mean, sure, it was hot, but not *that* hot.

> *"Hi Di, and it's mike. I hope things are going well for you and we have to all agreed. Now, there will be no newsletter and December, so that's really late but I would like to call I made for this week of the communications committee and I'm thinking that Wednesday evening and it's 7 o'clock and we're trying to keep it short. I'll send out an email a little bit here this afternoon but also some good news. Handeek leaving my husband. I've given up 500 dollar donation jail solve the cover the newsletter or however long that $500 less. So I think that's about the 6 about maybe four or five monthly payments. But anyway, I think them and I agreed to to to still pay for the Jenifer the issue, so I'll send you an email. Thanks very thing. I just want to get that word out to you about now newsletter this week. Okay, thanks."*

That, from my friend Mike who chairs a committee I'm on, still has me concerned for Handeek and his questionable relationship.

This next one is from Mary Ellen, our financial advisor's assistant. She calls my husband "Dad," so now I'm starting to look a little more closely at *that* relationship.

> *"Hi Dad, It's Tim, it's, Mary Ellen calling from D V D, and office Ameriprise and I was just calling to remind him of this conference call with the if it on Tuesday, January 12th at noon and they took him a call at that time. Okay, thanks very much and have a good day."*

This one might be from me calling home and leaving a message for my husband. I have a vague memory of saying "It's exhibits all day" or something similar. But I was not tired of walking around. I liked the walking around. And I can't think of anything more dangerous than a rejected mom doctor.

> *"Hi Mom, I mean rejected mom doctor or tired of walking around. It's exhibits all day. So anyway, it was just calling to check in. I might try your cell so talk to you later. Bye."*

I can't wait to hear what my doctor has to say when she calls next week with my blood test results.

Great-Grandma Is on Twitter and Other Signs the Rapture Is Near

I won't tell you how old my mother-in-law is. I'll just say that she has retired four times and has two great-grandchildren in high school. Also, her fingerprints wore off about five years ago, making it nearly impossible for her to be hired back at the school district where she had worked for forty years.

"We can't process your employment papers without a background check that includes fingerprints," they told her.

"Oh, for crying out loud, I'm [AGE DELETED] years old and I've worked here since the early 1970s. You kept hiring me to come back, remember? What do you think I did over the summer, hard time?"

The school board doesn't care that she's old enough to have complete layers of skin just disappearing from parts of her body. As long as she doesn't use those fingers to commit a felony, they'll keep begging her to come back and impart her wisdom on kids a fraction of her age.

They know she has the energy of their own grandchildren on Red Bull. And they know she's tech savvy enough to rock an IT job in the practical nursing department. She might be a wizard.

We knew she was a tech anomaly, but honestly, I thought it was just due to good job training. Teachers are forever having in-service days and going to training sessions at the county administration office, keeping their certifications up to date. There's always coffee, so of course everyone attends, my mother-in-law included.

But it wasn't until she used social media to track us down like dogs all the way across the country that I realized she's better at this than we are.

My husband and I were on a secret trip to San Francisco in 2012, a second-round job interview that we weren't allowed to talk about. I gave my husband a live-in-the-moment lecture before we left.

"No social media. No Twitter, no checking in, no look-everyone-I'm-at-the-airport, no Timothy-is-at-the-Golden-Gate-Bridge…" I ticked off his instructions for off-the-grid living while he packed. "No two cell phones with two different Facebook accounts blabbing about where you are. No Facebooking *at all*."

"Fine. I'm not stupid, you know," he huffed, stuffing device chargers into his suitcase as fast as I could take them out.

"I know you know this in your head, but get it into your heart: When you post as much as a thumbs-up on Facebook it shows where you are. And no photos *at all*," I said. "I'm pretty sure your iPhone auto-posts pictures to Instagram with your longitude-latitude coordinates."

I could see I was scaring him, so I tried to make a retro trip sound less Cro-Magnon and more fun.

"It'll be great! We'll stay off social media together. We can pretend we're on a secret mission where our assignment is to read paperback bestsellers and do the Jumble."

The first day of the trip, he got an A+. No phones, no Facebook, no Twitter. Not a single luxury. Then the long day of interviews was over and we were unwinding at a restaurant downtown. He had just ordered his second Manhattan and I went to the restroom. When I came back to the table, he was staring at his phone.

"Uh-oh."

When your reportedly off-the-grid husband says *uh-oh,* you know that he effed something up.

"What did you do?"

"It's my mom. She just DM'd me on Twitter and said *where r u?*"

"What did you do?"

"I didn't do anything! I just—I didn't do *anything.* I just liked this one little thing that your sister put on Facebook. This tiny little picture from your teeny tiny sister. One microscopic, newborn-baby *like.*"

"Yeah, and Facebook attached your location," I said. "What did I tell you?" I had half a mind to take away his cocktail and make him stand in time-out in the men's room.

I decided we could fix this by making up some story about how Facebook made an error, but my husband disagreed.

"She'll never buy it." He was probably right. His mother knows way more than she had been letting on. When she didn't hear back from him right away, she went social-media-gonzo and searched the Internet for reasons why we might be in San Francisco. She was one LinkedIn jobs board away from learning the reason for our trip when my husband finally spilled the beans.

After it was all out in the open and I had a chance to think about it, I asked my husband, "So your mom tweets?" I had seen the egg on her profile and figured she never waded into those twatters.

"Apparently," he said. Since then I've found out she follows Katie Couric, Ohio State football, NPR Politics, and the girls on the *Today* show. And her on-a-secret-mission son isn't the only person she DMs. She used Twitter to contact Tiger Woods and Dr. Sanjay Gupta about a blood therapy treatment the three of them know something about. She was disappointed neither of them DM'd her back. They probably don't know what DM means.

Meanwhile she's putting *Social Media Bloodhound* on her resume, for when the school district hires her back for the fifth time.

Facebook for Fifty and Over

As Facebook claws its way to the top spot in our list of things we love, more and more people my age are succumbing. Almost every day, someone my age gets a Facebook page. And another ounce of hope in a Gen Xer's brain dries up. Because it's been on a high-speed growth spurt since it was created, Facebook is not easy to pick up unless you've been with it from the beginning, especially for those of us fifty and older. Remember, we have a hard time learning languages and musical instruments too.

I think some lessons are in order just to save us fifty-and-over folks from embarrassment. I've convinced my kids and their high school and college friends that I'm hip enough to be their friend, but if you keep jabbering on about the '70s and posting pictures of skate keys, you're going to give us all a bad name.

1. Know your levels of dissing.

There are levels of getting rid of annoying people. If their status updates are irritating or go against your political philosophy to the point where you start to fantasize about a verbal confrontation with them at a face-to-face class reunion that could never happen in the real world, then you probably should hide them. No need for unfriending. They might convert or somehow be useful to you and a future evil plan you may come up with. You never know. Hiding doesn't hurt anyone and doesn't sound any alarms.

Unfriending tells the person you have no use for him now or ever. This may have to be repeated several times, since many people assume they were unfriended by mistake. "Facebook messed up again! I somehow dropped off your friends list!" You can blame Facebook the first time, but subsequent unfriendings require a backbone.

Blocking sends up red flags all over cyberspace. Don't even think about it. Blocking is for drama queens, paranoid schizophrenics, and people in the Witness Protection Program. If you block someone, they'll know it, as will everyone else, and you'll be forced to explain why you're such a dweeb. Don't go there.

2. There are no phones in Facebook.

Don't say "Who do I call about this?" if you're having problems with your Facebook account. You'll be able to hear the cringing of two hundred thousand twenty-somethings. Facebook wonks don't use telephones. Phones are barbaric and frankly an insult to the technology. And just for the record, a delayed poke is not a problem worth not calling about.

3. Learn to let go of your desire for privacy.

If you don't want anybody and everybody to know everything about you, then stay off Facebook. Don't join a social networking site and then complain that people are socially networking with you. Don't obsess over who is looking for you or who is checking you out. You put those photos of the block party on your page, what did you want to happen? If—God forbid—Facebook actually ever does allow you to see who's "stalking" you, you may be disappointed to find that it's no one. And stop worrying about everyone knowing your phone number and email address, because Facebook, that evil genius, revealed it without your permission. Everyone already knows your phone number and email address. That's why you get unwanted junk mail and solicitation calls from marketers. Embrace the intrusions.

4. Don't be Facebook-bullied into loving things.

Many older people seem to think that if you don't copy and paste the post on Daughter Day, Son Week, the Pledge of Allegiance, and Proud to Be a Christian, it means you don't love your family or your country or God. Nothing bad will happen if you don't repost. A quick and simple *like* does the trick and is effective in preventing bad things from raining down on your head.

5. No poking.

This one is just my opinion, but since this is my book I'm allowed to say it. Poking people is just as annoying as if someone actually poked you. I can't figure out why pokes are still on Facebook. It's amazing that they survived Black Death Hell September 2011, when Facebook changes drove hundreds of people to suicidal thoughts, self-medicating, and threats to go Amish. It's possibly a vast Facebook conspiracy.

6. Stop complaining.

We all agree that Facebook is evil for a) selling our private information so that advertisers can stalk us in the most cyber-creepy way, b) not bowing to pressure to create a dislike button, c) constantly changing, and d) not giving a rat's ass how we would run Facebook if we'd had the foresight to invent a world-changing social media.

But complaining about the changes as if you were an expert on the *old* Facebook is just annoying.

The constant changing, improving, and tweaking may indeed drive you bat-shit crazy, but please try to stop being so whiny. Sure, Facebook knows that we fifty-plus-ers are going to be its bread and butter well after younger, hipper people find something else. And they are aware that we don't handle change very well. (People my age didn't handle it well when their IBM Selectrics were carted off and replaced with those giant computers, either. But they survived.) They are not going to stop changing Facebook. I repeat: They are NOT going to stop making changes to Facebook. Try to keep up.

7. Not to be a grammar nerd, but I'm going to have to say something about spelling and punctuation.

No, you don't have to be self-conscious about your horrible English. That is, unless you post Michael Savage quotes about illegals who have the nerve not to study the English language and then, yes, you better dust off that Strunk & White. (I wasn't going to say anything, but some of you are making our Guatemalan lawn workers sound like Edwin Newman.)

Leaving out punctuation, a common Facebook thing to do, can cause misunderstanding, and also people will hate to read your posts. I've sometimes had to read a post three times, once aloud, to figure out what the point is. *LOL Krissy are you back if your down this way give us a shout just recovered from sunday night out with ray tomorrow.* That's just too much work for what little information I'm getting. A couple of commas and a semicolon wouldn't kill you.

But as long as you're willing to take the risks, don't worry too, too much about grammar on Facebook. With one exception: Be sure to get your own name right. I keep seeing a friend suggestion for a guy who didn't capitalize his own first name. Unless you're a beat poet or an artist living in the Village, if you see that you screwed up your own name, remember: You can fix it.

8. Be the few, the proud, the 3 percent.

Younger, shallower Facebookers will steadily pelt you with sulky taunts. "Put this on your profile for at least one hour today. 97 percent of you won't do it, but I think I know which of my friends will." They don't really know which of their friends will post it. They're not even going to check. They're just saying that. Remember, it's not like refusing to throw a buck into the hat for a birthday gift for a co-worker or funeral flowers. This is not a moment where you have to think about your image or what people will think of you. It's more like getting that cheesy junk mail from the FOP with pictures of crippled kids on the envelope, trying to make you feel ashamed to use the complimentary address labels or the nickel taped to a card if you don't send them $50. You don't fall for that, so don't fall for Facebook extortion.

My Facebook friends probably don't know that I am actually against middle school bullying, cancer, and terrorism, and I do support autistic kids, mothers who have lost their children, soldiers, and Jesus. I just don't feel obligated to use my Facebook page to announce it. If you start reposting everything that you're shamed into reposting, you'll soon find out there are a lot more diseases and levels of human misery than you can imagine. You'll be working overtime just to keep up with Facebook repostings. Set a precedent early by not reposting anything, no matter how much you support it. Be strong. It gets easier.

9. Contain your joy over all the crushes, sagas, and blitzes.

In two months, replace the names of the above games with whatever the hot Facebook games are. And then two months after that, replace them again.

I'm not saying don't play these games. Games are fun and purposeful. Ever since *A Beautiful Mind*, I stopped feeling guilty about games I play. If a brainiac like John Nash can devote his life to the mathematics of gaming, who am I not to play hours of Tetris every day?

Play away! But resist the urge to send all of your friends invitations to join you. We know it's a blast. We know how you get into it and it's a cheap, non-alcoholic way to unwind. We know you've made lots of friends because of it. But if we wanted to play, we would play. We wouldn't wait for a third or fourth invitation.

10. It counts.

Facebook is now an acceptable method for:

- thank-you notes
- party invitations
- engagement announcements
- engagement breakoffs
- telling your husband that you're going to be late for dinner
- finding a Realtor

In other words, doing it on Facebook makes it count now. This isn't just some toy-of-the-month, people. Facebook is serious stuff. I know two relationships that are the result of Facebook romances, so it can change your life.

11. Don't be inappropriate.

I know this is nebulous since everyone's standards for "inappropriate" are different. The Facebook Status Update website is no help; it advises that you should not post "anything you wouldn't stand up on a chair and shout in the pub." I can't imagine what *could* be appropriate shouted from atop a chair in a pub. You'd obviously be very drunk if you were doing that, and everything you said might be inappropriate. Just think about the post for a second before you hit "Share." While you're proofreading it (hint, hint) ask yourself, "Should I be sending this out there for my coworkers/kids' friends/dental hygienist/junior high boyfriend to see?" Take a glance through your featured friends in the left margin. How will they react? And then hit "Share" anyway. You're halfway to the grave. Live a little.

Well, Isn't That Pinteresting

My husband is all hepped up on social media, to the point where he wants to be the first to try whatever comes across his computer screen. So when he asked me about Pinterest, I told him it was for girls.

"Really? Just girls?"

"Yep. Just girls. Everything's all pink and ruffly and shabby chic and country French over there," I told him, hoping those keywords would scare him off. I know for a fact that *country French* causes him to run to the garage and guzzle a Bud Light.

Pinterest is the only place I've got where no one in my immediate family notices how much time I'm wasting. If my husband gets on Pinterest, I won't have anything shallow I can call my own.

I don't know why I want to spend so much time over there. Pinterest is supposed to make you want to be a better person. For me, it's a self-esteem killer.

For every good recipe I find, I get another piece of evidence that I'm not as fashionable, as rich, or as tall as what seems to be every other woman on the planet. I had no idea how low on the skank-o-meter I was until I started looking at everyone else's boards.

Thanks to Pinterest, I now know the following:

My nails are not colorful and designy enough

Even when I get a manicure I pick a solid color nail polish in the red/pink family. Unless you're going to have fingertips painted like a red-and-white checkered tablecloth with ants crawling across them, why bother, really?

I don't know how to dress myself

I don't wear enough matching shoes with my outfits. Also my sunglasses are not big enough to complete an ensemble. And my thighs, which are wider than my ankles, are huge.

I can't make shit

There are millions of women more creative than me. And I'm not just talking about making cupcakes using fondant so it doesn't look like Spanky and Our Gang got their hands on some Play-Doh. I mean women who make their own leather purses, build chandeliers out of mason jars, and crochet everything from earrings to beanbag chairs. This one lady makes her own bras. If you think an apple cozy is weird, know that on Pinterest there are several *hundred* different types of apple cozies. I had no idea the apples were cold.

I'm not crunchy enough

I don't even know where to buy burlap in bulk. Before Pinterest I didn't think that mattered. I've always considered myself semi-earthy and somewhat of a do-it-yourselfer, but when I saw a pin on how to make your own buttons, I said, *really?* Sorry uber-crafters, but I can't imagine a world in which I would get satisfaction out of wearing a shirt with buttons I had hand-forged out of polymer. Unless it was a huge button that said, "I MAKE MY OWN BUTTONS. HUZZAH!"

I used to send a little note and link to my brother-in-law Dan every time I saw something made out of wine corks. Pinterest put an end to that. The Internet can't handle the traffic required to show Dan all the things people are making after polishing off a bottle of wine. He's just going to have to put his manhood on a back burner and get himself on this site.

I'm not deep enough

There's a lot of sappy crap on Pinterest. Not as much as Facebook, but enough to keep the men away. It can be nauseating, even for a real girl like me. But the day I see a picture of a young Ali McGraw with the words "Love means never having to say you're sorry" in a script font is the day I close up my board and move to Spike.com. I think my husband is already over there. And he has a drink waiting for me. And it's not in a glass hand-painted to look like a giant candy corn.

Technology - Infinity; Diane - 0

The technology in my house is kicking my butt. Honestly, if the communications accoutrement team in my home and I were in the ring, it would be delivering Jackie Chan roundhouse kicks to my groin and I'd be curled up in a fetal position protecting my head with *The Complete Works of William Shakespeare* and a newspaper.

It's in a 'Vette on the Autobahn and I'm in a Barbie car stuck in a funeral procession, behind an Amish buggy and a tractor.

It's president of the class, captain of the football team, and the lead in the play, and I'm leaving my locker lock fake-closed because I can't remember the combination.

I think you get the picture.

My husband has been wanting a new computer, and I'm dreading the moment something happens that we have enough money to buy one. Because it will shine a light on how much I already don't know what I'm doing. I'm faking it well, but only because I've memorized which buttons to push. When on the phone with tech support or in any conversation with my husband outside the bedroom, I crumble because I don't know when I last emptied my cache of cookies.

"As delicious as that sounds, I'm not quite sure I remember. How full would it have been, and where would I have dumped it?" I asked the Apple guy. "Is it possible that I ate them?"

While my computer-related possessions are in first place in the race to make me look stupid, my telephone technology runs a close second. We now have three home phone numbers from three different sources, which may not sound like a lot, except for the fact that we rarely use the house phone. It never rings. We get all our calls on our individual cell phones.

Despite that, my husband has fallen in love with Magic Jack (no relation to Magic Johnson; and while we're on the subject, why is his name not the punchline in more dirty jokes?). Magic Jack is a small device that looks like a prop from *Mission Impossible*, something that could stealthily be passed to a woman in a tightly cinched trench coat on a dark Berlin street, mostly because it has a clear front that shows a bunch of little squares and other blue, high-tech things inside there. It provides you with (no, not the secret recipe for making a bomb) a phone number that you can use to call anywhere in the world.

It is simple enough that my husband had to take it one step further and route it through a Google phone number and then forward our original home number to the Magic Jack and—oh man. When the phone rings, I answer it and what else matters? Especially since it hardly ever rings?

If we get the new computer, everything is going to get kicked up a notch. I believe that household technology is enmeshed in a symbiotic relationship where each component feeds off the others' success. The phones will start answering themselves and making return calls, signing us up for flood insurance, putting me down for brownies at the band bake sale, and answering the Republicans' surveys about how disappointed we aren't in Barack Obama's administration.

I'm going to just let techno-nature take its course and do with me what it will. I'll be here, eating my cookies, so the cache doesn't get full.

Skype, Skype Me Baby

When my oldest son first started making noise about moving to China, my mom-worry-o-meter went to Red Level 4 with all the things I feared for him. I worried about him getting into a stranger's van, thinking it was a Chinese taxi. I worried about him trying to pose from the top of the Great Wall and getting blown off by high winds. I worried about him eating things with tentacles on a dare. And I worried about him getting sick and not knowing enough Chinese to tell the doctor to use modern medicine to cure him and not acupressure.

What I didn't worry about was not being able to see him for a year at a time.

Except for the high winds, those other things did actually happen. What also happened was that I went into a near panic when I realized I wasn't going to see him until his first visit home in thirteen months.

"You've got to get Skype," my high school friend Jim told me.

I had not yet heard of Skype, which was in its infancy at the time. Jim, who lived in the Czech Republic, had sent both of his sons to college in the States and claims that the only reason he could bear that heart-wrenching piece of parenting was because we now had things from *The Jetsons*.

"You'll love it," Jim said, "because you can see them and talk to them just like they're sitting across from you."

Skype is how I learned that in China the heat is turned off in all buildings on a preset date, regardless of a late cold snap in the spring, and turned back on in all buildings on a preset date, regardless of a young American guy whose nose has turned blue.

"Are you wearing a winter coat?" I asked my son as we Skyped one day. He was sitting in his living room.

"Yeah, the heat's been turned off but it's still pretty cold out," he said.

"Well, can't you complain to your landlord?" I asked, clueless that when your landlord is the Ministry of Put a Sweater on Comrade, that's not really an option.

Yes, I learned more about his life in China via Skype than a long string of phone conversations could possibly allow. When he got a dog, I knew it wasn't working out even before I asked "How is the dog working out?" There was a hole in his favorite sweater, his glasses were taped together, and he looked exhausted. The dog wouldn't make an appearance, but I knew he was nearby, since my son's left arm kept jerking downward.

"You're trying to pet him, aren't you?" I asked.

"The dog's not really working out," he said. As it turns out, he was trying to strangle the dog.

Score another one for Skype.

I think it's great that video chats are no longer only for people in sci-fi movies, *Twilight Zone* episodes, and Mr. Spacely's video conferences on the days that George worked from home.

Skype is now another arrow in the quiver of parents everywhere, and not just when their kids move to a foreign country. Skype is perfect for parents of college kids who think they chose a school far away enough that they don't have to put up with their moms meddling, nagging, and incessantly asking, "Are you sure a parent will be there?"

You want to see what your kid's dorm room looks like when his mother isn't there to gather up the empty Gatorade bottles that litter his floor. And those better be Gatorade bottles, mister.

For now I'm limiting my Skyping to my own offspring and others who have seen me at the pre-surgery prep level of makeuplessness. I've seen my own face on the Skype screen and it's not exactly forgiving. When the camera first pops up on the screen, if your screen is tilted just so, you'll look like you're peering down into your own grave.

The better to intimidate your independent children with.

Five

GIVE IT TO ME STRAIGHT, DOC

Skin Deep Is Still Pretty Deep

I went to the dermatologist for the first time since I had acne as a teenager. I had to be checked for moles, which is not unlike being checked for tics by a mother monkey, except you get to have a paper blanket covering parts of you at all times. And there are no bananas.

Dermatologists used to be for teenagers with acne. Now they're for older people who want their wrinkles to disappear and their faces to be plumper and less expressive. The people who just want to make sure they don't have a cancery mole have never held a place of honor among dermatologists. We barely pay the light bill.

How much has dermatology changed in thirty-five years? When I went to one for acne treatments in the early 1970s, I a) was given a prescription for vitamins; b) was told not to eat pizza, chocolate, and potato chips; and c) got zapped with radioactive rays. The only sign that anyone in the office thought that might be a little bit unsafe was the fact that I had to wear goggles to protect my eyes.

I had terrible skin. My mom first took me to our family doctor. Dr. Martin's specialty was not acne, but giving penicillin shots and handing out suckers. He took one look at my ravaged face and said, "You have the largest pores I've ever seen." And then he sent me to see Dr. Brody, a super-elderly dermatologist whose office was in downtown Youngstown.

My acne-riddled skin and possibly the freakish size of my pores sent Dr. Brody to the hospital in an ambulance on my first visit. I'm not kidding. My mom made me wear a skirt because we were going downtown and that was the rule. We went up to a very high floor of the Mahoning Bank Building and waited about an hour in the waiting room of Dr. Brody's office. We eventually got called into Dr. Brody's tiny, dark little office, where we sat across from his desk and he told me my acne would require weekly light treatments, a daily vitamin and antibiotic, and a strict diet of everything that wasn't chocolate, pizza, and potato chips.

Then he pushed back his chair, stood up, and said, "I'll go get some samples and a brochure for you. I'll be right back."

About twenty-five minutes later Dr. Brody still hadn't returned and we were getting annoyed. The office was really quiet. People had stopped walking past the door. After about forty-five minutes, we saw a receptionist sprint by the doorway. Then, very quietly, two guys walked by carrying a stretcher.

Another receptionist walked past and saw us sitting there in the office, looking sideways and wondering what was going to pass by the doorway next.

"Oh, are you still here?" she squawked when she saw us. "Dr. Brody had a heart attack." She was visibly upset. She shoved some sample acne cream tubes and prescriptions and brochures into my hands, said "Don't eat pizza!" and pushed us toward the door.

"Did he say anything about what caused the first chest pain?" I wanted to ask. "Anything about my pores?"

The next week I went back for my first acne treatment and was seen by Dr. Brody's partner, Dr. Cukerbaum, who was to be my dermatologist for the next three years. Sadly, Dr. Brody never returned to the medical practice.

Every Saturday for a couple of years I had to go back to the Mahoning Bank Building and put goggles on and get ray beams blasted onto my face. I semi-religiously took my vitamins and semi-unreligiously avoided pizza, chocolate, and potato chips.

The weekly visits are like a bad dream to me now. Dermatology seemed like a racket. They'd tell you that you had to come every week to get the death rays, but you didn't have an appointment. You would just wait, all stacked up, until you got called. It was a couple of hours every Saturday out of my life and, more importantly, I realize now, out of my mother's life. Why on earth didn't she raise holy hell and say, "Blast my daughter's face right now so we can get out of here and get to McKelvey's Loft! There are polyester tops just sitting there while we waste valuable downtown shopping time!"

There were so many people waiting for their light treatments, sometimes the waiting room was SRO with pimply teenagers and we had to sit on the floor of the hall outside, which was quickly stacking up with more pimply teenagers. Occasionally you'd see an older person with impetigo or leprosy, eczema, or what we now know as rosacea, but back then was Gross Skin That's All Red. To us pimply-faced teenagers, these people were fascinating because they had a skin condition that was at least different from ours. Plus, they had real appointments.

Today's dermatologist's office has almost no pimply teenagers. It's full of people with perfect skin waiting to get their Botox injections. The office itself is wall-to-wall posters of famous people advertising an injection that keeps you wrinkle free and working in Hollywood for four to six months.

Even I was tricked into buying something in a pump bottle that cost $64 that the doctor said I had to have to prevent skin cancer, but would make me look prettier as a side benefit.

If I do get skin cancer, how much do you want to bet it has something to do with those death rays I got zapped with years ago? How can I complain? My acne is gone.

A Run-In with the Doctor

I knew this would happen. While on the bleachers at a high school soccer game, I saw the doctor who gave me my colonoscopy. I had just been telling someone that I haven't lived here long enough to run into people I know in the store or around town. I'm still new and unfriendly enough that I could run into Starbucks in a pajama top, wearing my husband's flip flops, with greasy hair, glasses, and my retainer, and it wouldn't come back to bite me. The strangers would just think I'm a regular ugly person, possibly mentally ill for my clothing choices, but it wouldn't reflect back on Diane Fitzpatrick, neighbor and soccer mom.

So I was at a soccer game, and one of the players got injured and this guy got up from the stands and walked down and started acting like a doctor, and I went *uh-oh*. It was my colon doctor.

It ticks me off that I even have a colon doctor. I was ticked when I found out that just because I was fifty I had to have this disgusting test done. And I first had to have a consultation with the doctor who was going to do the procedure.

I would have preferred to be far more anonymous with the colon doctor, but the receptionist insisted. I met with him briefly. He seemed like a very nice person, despite his poor job choice. (I think they keep these poor med students up for ninety-six hours straight and then have them fill out the form to choose a specialty.)

But I really never, ever thought I'd see him again after the whole disgusting thing was over. I plan to have a very healthy colon from now until I die, because I'm never going through that again. In fact I'm refusing to do any kind of fasting or clear liquids diet ever. I don't care what I'm being tested for; if the medical technology is so unsophisticated that they can't beam through Honey Bunches of Oats and coffee to find what they're looking for, then I'll just wait. In one of the later *Star Trek* movies, McCoy time-travels back to the late '80s and walks through a hospital, curing people with a wave of a small flashing, beeping piece of plastic. I'll wait for that.

Back to the soccer game: The colon doctor hung around the injured player for a while and then watched the rest of the game near the fence. I glanced over at him once, and I think he was looking my way and recognized me. I was afraid to stand up for fear he'd see my butt and go, "Oh, yeah, that's her!" I silently cursed my decision to never wear a burka. I avoided him, and when the game was over I walked all around the bleachers to get to my car and quickly sped away.

Then I started to wonder, what about all the helpers? There were at least two nurses standing there when the drugs took effect and I passed out (one of them had a little grin on her face, which I did not like), plus the anesthesiologist, his assistant, and God knows who else. The place was a bustling mecca, and I'm not even certain they closed the door. They probably all live nearby. As far as I know, my kids' English teacher and the president of my homeowners' association were invited in to watch. That's really why they knock you out for these procedures. They don't want you to know who has seen you naked and in a demeaning position.

I can't really think about it too much or I'll never make any friends here. I'm going to have to let it go. And get a pair of those big Nicole Richie sunglasses.

Let's Get Physical

It's that time of year again—time to fill out the health assessment so employers can find out personal things about their employees' private lives and use them to make judgments about people's livelihoods. The Tea Party can just shut up about the Obama White House sticking its nose into our personal health decisions: This has been going on long before the liberals snapped on a pair of rubber gloves.

I was surprised to see the reminder in my inbox. Didn't I just take the health assessment? Yup, I just took it in January. And I took it the September before that. It seems for every continent's New Year and possibly Rosh Hashanah, we have to retake the health assessment, just so everyone can be cleared of having slipped into a state of risky and unhealthy behaviors.

Because I'm married to whom I'm married to, the health assessment is another competition in our house.

"What did you score?" my husband asked me after the first time we took it.

"I don't know, but I think I did pretty good," I answered.

"What? You didn't look at your score?" He couldn't believe that I hadn't even tried to nudge my numbers up by exaggerating how much sweat I generate when I do yard work. A lot of the time it's water from the hose, let's be honest.

So I looked back at my score and it was in the 90s. I thought that was good. Better than his anyway.

But I couldn't help but try to gain a few points in subsequent tests. I knew he would be working hard to get his score up, and if he did better than me the result would be constant taunting that could be hazardous to someone's health, ironically causing a dip in scores.

Eventually I did score a 100. This time I was at 98, but I think I have a couple of things working against me.

- I didn't know my blood pressure this time. I thought about running into Publix and sitting down at that self-serve blood pressure chair, but that thing scares me. When the cuff starts to tighten around my arm without a human at the other end of it, I get a jolt of anxiety that it's going to just keep squeezing and not let up, leaving me to seek help from the guy who slices deli meat. Plus, the grocery store blood pressure machine has me looking straight at the rectal thermometers and reading glasses—not a combination conducive to a nice, slow, steady heartbeat.
- I used to drive an SUV but now I drive a compact or subcompact car. I can only imagine that driving a Prius is considered taking your life in your hands whenever you get behind the wheel. At least on the Florida highways.
- I don't have a job and I had to check *Unemployed,* which I'm guessing is a health bummer. There were only the two choices, though, or I would have checked *Independently wealthy* or *Kept woman* or *Doesn't really feel like working right now but I'm doing OK thanks for caring.*

Some of the questions are no-brainers. I floss *Every day,* I wear sunscreen or adequate clothing *All the time,* I am *Completely satisfied* with my life, and I have *Very strong* social ties with my family and/or friends. I sleep *Well* and I feel *Completely refreshed* half an hour after getting up in the morning. I get all possible screenings and tests every single year, but I haven't spent any time in the ER in the past twelve months. All those questions I'm sure added to my pointage.

But others are trickier. "What is the highest level of education you have achieved?" Are blue-collar workers unhealthier than white-collar? Did we learn some health tips at college graduation that people with some college didn't get? And what about income level? Does that matter? Are the rich healthier than the poor? Even now, with healthcare reform, where we're all equal and the death panels are disposing of all the sick old people as fast as they can?

I'd love to go back and change some answers then reconfigure, just to see what makes the difference in my health assessment score. But I'm afraid of screwing around with this test like I've done with other online surveys. When I took the Real Age test I kept retaking it, entering more outrageous lifestyle choices to see what it would take to be a fifty-year-old whose Real Age is twenty-five. Turns out I would have to eat my body weight in pure fiber, whole grains, and raw vegetables, exercise both weight-bearing and cardio for six hours a day, and listen to a better radio station.

The health assessment competition between my husband and me is secondary to the one he has going with one of his co-workers. She's always throwing her 100s in his face. However, I know for a fact that she jumped out of an airplane a few months ago, so I wonder how she'll score this year. As long as she wore her seat belt on the drive to the air strip, I think she'll be okay.

Mono-a-Mono Vision, I Heart You

I'm a thirty-seven-year contact lens wearer. I first wore contacts when they were like Barbie-car headlights that you pushed into your eyes, and if you left them on there a half-hour too long, you'd end up in the ER with gauze pads taped to your eyes. Only when they were banned in all but Third World countries did I begrudgingly give them up and move to gas-permeable hard lenses. I agreed to switch to soft, disposable lenses only when I heard there were crafts you could do with the old ones. I had a hard time with the concept of throwing away your lenses after two weeks. I was also struggling with disposable razors and sour cream containers.

As a result, my corneas are like that unrippable plastic sheeting that old people used to put on their sofas. I am one tough old broad when it comes to my peepers.

But you should have seen how scared I was when I tried mono-vision contact lenses for the first time last week. I've got them on a trial basis, to see how it goes in anticipation of having mono-vision LASIK surgery. I was more afraid of trying the mono-vision lenses than I am of the surgery itself. And the surgery involves props from *A Clockwork Orange* and lasers.

For those of you who aren't up on vision-speak, mono vision is when you need help seeing distance, and because you're now old, you need help reading and seeing things close-up too. Mono-vision glasses, contacts, and LASIK surgery has you seeing out of one eye for distance and the other eye for close-up.

"Your brain will adapt and pretty soon your eyes will know which one is supposed to work, depending on where you're looking." That's what I was told.

The concept of mono vision, the brain in general, and why I need to put on reading glasses on top of contact lenses are three related mysteries to me. I wasn't really unhappy doing it my way but was worn down by my husband, who had mono-vision LASIK surgery earlier this year, and you would have thought he had been given Colonel Steve Austin's eyes.

I put it off as long as possible and then I went for my consult last week.

I can't explain why I was nervous about it. Maybe because I was afraid I wouldn't be able to handle seeing mono-a-mono, and then I'd have to admit that my brain is inferior to my husband's brain, which adapted swimmingly. I had heard that some people can't do it.

"You'll know right away," Andrea from the eye doctor's office said. "If you get up and start to walk and you get dizzy and nauseated, you'll know you can't do it."

"But maybe if that happens, I'll just have to keep trying. Maybe I'll get used to them." I was pathetically trying to be hopeful. You don't understand, I wanted to say, my husband and I are very competitive. I'm doing this if I have to get a walker and strap an emesis basin to my wrist.

"Nah, you'll know right away." Andrea is all business.

I was so scared, but I put them in. No dizziness. No nausea. I drove home and didn't hit anything.

Then I started to realize what my husband had been so ga-ga over all this time. I sat down at the computer and didn't have to find a pair of reading glasses to see the type on the screen. I was able to walk to the mailbox and read the mail.

Taking pictures! I ran to my closet and got out my camera. I took a picture, then looked down at the tiny settings and could read them.

Piano! I ran over to the piano, sat down, and played a little of "The Shadow of Your Smile" without readers. I could see the music notes and the keys.

Oh my God, books! Picked up *The Plague* and read a paragraph in bad lighting without reading glasses and without holding it across the room. I did get a little bit nauseated then, but that book is gross.

Knitting! I can see the stitches and look up and see Jack McCoy scrunch up his face in that multiuse smile-scowl expression he is so good at.

Recipes! I can read the fine print. Shopping! I can look at an entire outfit and read the price tag without fumbling in my purse for glasses. Restaurants! I could read the menu without donating a $20 pair of reading glasses to the busboy by leaving my token pair on the table between the candle and the ketchup.

This is very exciting. Now that I've got my big fear out of the way, the actual surgery is going to be a piece of cake.

I'll be able to read the bill and flee the jurisdiction.

Happy Hour Is Officially Over

I had to have a spur-of-the-moment, unscheduled physical because I got a new doctor. I separated from my old doctor, who kept telling me I was fine. Cholesterol is 249? No problem! You're great! That blip on your EKG that keeps getting rounder and uglier every year? Don't sweat it. Old Doctor unwittingly encouraged me to keep doing whatever I was doing.

"I don't have a single health problem, and I'm not on any medications!" I would brag at parties, with cheese log stuffed in my cheeks and a tumbler full of wine in my hand. Then I switched doctors.

Happy hour is officially over. So is going to the gym without a half-gallon of water. And bring on the maxi-sized pill case, because I'll now be on all those supplements so popular with people my age.

New Doctor is not about to take all the blame for this drastic change in my lifestyle. He got all of my medical records from Old Doctor then copied them and emailed them to me. And that was the first time I ever saw with my own eyes all of my test results and all the things the doctor wrote down during my exams.

Holy crap. I had been careening toward an early death and had no idea. Eating out, drinking every day, eating cupcake frosting out of the bowl with a spoon, cracking jokes throughout my physicals with Old Doctor… And all the while my "numbers" were going up (or down, whichever is the bad way) and nobody thought to tell me. It's all fun and games until someone has to have a colonoscopy.

Most of what she wrote down was positive. She said I was age appropriate, well nourished, and my mood was appropriate to the situation. I'm taking all that as a compliment and not that I was dressing like a slut.

I was oriented to person, place, and time with no confusion noted. Seeing as I am often running late and forget which pharmacy I use, I'm pretty proud of that one. They made no mention of the fact that when I exited the examining room, I never knew which way to turn to get back to reception, even though I'd been a patient there for four years. Bad sense of direction and faulty short-term memory were not recorded.

But even some of the good things sounded pretty horrid. The picture of health isn't a pretty visual when you're forced to use medical jargon. I was shocked at how aged, puffy, and diseased my internal organs sounded. Her report went through my whole body and made it sound like a lumpy, pulsating hunk of lard.

My head was normocephalic, atraumatic, without any gross head or neck masses.

My turbinates revealed no abnormalities, but my oropharynx and posterior pharynx revealed pink, moist, patent tissues without mass or erythema. That just sounds like borderline porn.

No bruits were ansculated.

She felt no murmurs, gallop, rubs, or clicks.

No clubbing. I don't think I'm supposed to take that as an order, but I'm going to avoid the bars, just to cover all bases.

Bowel sounds present x4. (Times 4? Doesn't that seem loud? That can't be good.)

On my blood work, I was negative on occult (which I think is good; you never want the occult in your bod) and no squamous cells were seen (also good . . . yeah, let's just say that's good).

I'm third generation on my TSH, which is probably more evolved and hipper than first generation.

None of these things were the problem, though. Old Doctor didn't write down anything bad, she just let the lab results tell the story . . . to no one. And New Doctor is quite the man of action, because he read those results and started making lists of things for me to do. Unfortunately, none of my newly revealed health issues have anything to do with inherited tendencies. It's all stuff that I can, should, and must (New Doctor says) work to improve. Dammit.

I promised him that I had already started to make some changes. He said he would run another set of labs, and then he'd let me know if I can still have my one precious glass of wine every night. But the cereal bowl of frosting is out.

About as Funny as a Root Canal

Throughout my adult life I've lived a charmed existence when it comes to dental work. When I was in my twenties I had a few fillings. In my thirties I had a crown, a root canal, and a wisdom teeth extraction. In my forties I had a second crown and adult braces. None of these were particularly painful, except for the braces, which I can't talk about yet or I'll cry. Give me another two or three years and maybe I can describe how upset I am that in the twenty-first century we are still straightening teeth by slowly turning screws on a series of tiny vises. The point is, I didn't have any real horror stories stemming from dentistry. I got my teeth cleaned, checked, and X-rayed like clockwork every six months. Like I said: charmed.

My childhood wasn't as rosy. Our family dentist had a bad attitude and worse personal hygiene. To this day the smell of Brylcreem and halitosis makes me clench my teeth shut and run. My baby teeth wouldn't fall out so most of them had to be pulled to make room for permanent teeth that would soon be filled with molten lead, which would then turn from silver to black, making me look gross in all pictures where I'm laughing. If I asked, "Do I have something in my teeth?" the answer was, Yes, 12 ounces of black steel.

My childhood experience helped set in stone my determination to get regular checkups. If I had a dentist look in my mouth every six months, I reasoned, there wouldn't be time for something horrible to happen. We would nip it in the bud.

Then last week I had to get a root canal. I wouldn't go so far as to call it an emergency root canal, but I had an hour's notice.

In that hour, I had to choose between getting a shower or finishing up a freelance article that was due in a couple hours. I chose the shower. In retrospect, I should have finished the article. Only hours after walking into the endodontist's office, I was covered in my own spit, sweat, and tears. My deodorant hadn't as much worn off as died by assassination in a blitzkrieg of perspiration, and my makeup had retreated into my inner beauty. I felt like a fool for having spritzed on some cologne before leaving the house.

I understand root canals about as much as I understand orthodontics, which is somewhere between nothing and wrong. I listened patiently as Dr. Yee explained how he was going to do the root canal. I resisted the temptation to ask even a single question because it might show my vast void of knowledge about teeth, their roots and nerves, gums, my jaw—pretty much everything south of my nose and north of my turkey gobbler.

Based on Dr. Yee's explanation—which included an ice cream cone analogy that started out cute but ended up leaving me confused, hungry, and worried about the cracked cone leaking melted ice cream all over the floor—I think I've figured out how root canals work.

They work this way: First he puts you in a rubber mask direct from Quentin Tarantino's personal *Pulp Fiction* collection, and then he very carefully tries to shove cotton balls and silverware down your throat. You would do as directed and raise your hand "if you feel any discomfort," but then he'd see the middle finger you're flashing under your giant bib.

He puts goggles on you just for his own amusement. Every time there was a chance of splashing water or spit or stray shrapnel from the blowtorch, he would say "Close your eyes!" in a cheerful voice. As if when I opened them there would be a blue Tiffany box with a bow sitting on my stomach.

Afterward, they let me go to the restroom, but my hands were shaking so much I could hardly work the key. I got a glimpse of myself in the mirror. After four hours of having my mouth stretched open, I looked like the Joker, and not colorful, campy Cesar Romero, but creepy Heath Ledger. That was only one-half of my mouth. The other half was in a teeth-clenching frown.

"What's the deal?" I asked Dr. Yee's assistant when I got back in the chair. "Why are root canals still done like this? Isn't there a laser or something they can use to zap tooth nerves while we take a pill and go off into the Matrix for a while?"

And speaking of a pill, what happened to nitrous oxide? Valium? I got nothing. Not even Jerry Springer on a ceiling TV.

"There is some work being done on lasers, but it's still a few years down the road," the assistant said. "And as for nitrous, it sometimes can make the patient less cooperative."

I've decided to return to my charmed life and avoid all root canals until they improve the technology. I want music, I want lasers, I want visuals of puppies romping in a meadow playing in my brain, and when I open my eyes, I want a little blue box.

Competing in the Pink-Eye Event

I'm one of those people who only watches the Olympics to see the ice dancers get pushed to the brink and plot each others' kneecap injuries. So I didn't think I was missing much by skipping the Winter Olympics in Sochi.

And then Bob Costas got pink eye and I had to rethink my television viewing habits.

Not that I enjoy seeing someone suffer from the most unattractive illness next to leprosy. I myself had a pretty severe eye infection a couple of years ago, so I can relate to Bob and his disgusting eye. I really wanted to see Bob's eye infection to a successful conclusion—that conclusion being a return to his dignified career and to stop grossing everyone out.

At least he got to explain to millions of people around the world why he was wearing his glasses and his face was all messed up. When I had my eye infection, I didn't have an international audience, and the people I did see were too polite to ask what was up with the grody eye. Believe me, I'd have preferred a rude question blurted out. Then I could have explained that I had an official eye infection, diagnosed by a real doctor who went to medical school, who ordered me not to wear my contact lenses or mascara; in fact, I couldn't keep any makeup on my face at all because there was a constant stream of tears running down my blush-and-bronzer zone. But because no one asked, I looked like a homely drug addict with a common cold who had just been dumped by her boyfriend.

You only have to type in *Bob Co* in the Google search line before you get results like *Bob Costas eye infection gross blech ew icky.* That's because eye infections are the worst.

Mine lasted about six months. It happened to be at the time my daughter was auditioning at music schools, so I was traveling and reuniting with old friends who lived in town. It was winter too, and we were traveling in the frigid North from Florida, where I didn't even own a pair of closed-toe shoes. My red puffy eyes, tear tracks, and glasses were offset only by the outdated, ill-fitting winter clothes and shoes I was wearing.

In Indiana I got together with my husband's cousin, who I was meeting in person for the first time. In Cleveland I saw more people that I knew than strangers. By the time we got to New York, we met up with my niece, who was in town with half of her dad's family and her new boyfriend. The reunions and first impressions were racking up for me. Lots of photos were taken. And I had the eyes of someone just days away from a junkie's sad, lonely death.

That and the glasses. I know glasses are the accessory of the decade, and everyone's favorite perpetual hipster, Johnny Depp, wears empty frames even though he has 20/20 vision, but I didn't have those kind of glasses. I had the on-sale-at-Lens-Crafters glasses, the whatever-my-pathetic-vision-insurance-will-pay-for glasses, which had lost both rubbery nosepiece cushions and hurt to be on my face. I waited for the "Does your face hurt?" joke because I would have cut it off at the pass by saying, "Yes, actually my face *does* hurt, thank you very much."

Bob Costas explained the appearance of his glasses by using an old cartoon reference: "I have no choice but to go all Peabody & Sherman on you for the next couple of nights," he said. I cringed and let out a little moan, and I was joined by every woman who ever had nightmares about having to wear her glasses in her own wedding.

I feel for the guy. He had a public stage from which to explain away his red eyes and glasses, but he'll forever be known as The Eye Infection Guy. His eye was the number one trending topic on Google, his left eye had its own Twitter account, and the infection went viral—both ways.

He did make it back to Sochi, though, just in time to remind us that under normal, non-pink-eye conditions, he's not bad looking.

Six

I Enjoy Being a Girl, Overpriced Hair Products and All

The Only Clubbing I Do on Friday Nights

I'm in a book club! As a fifty-something this is only the second book club I've belonged to, so you get some idea of what a trend follower I am. It also tells you something about my social life that we meet on Friday nights and that will now be my most thrilling thing to do on Friday nights.

My new book club is for smart people who like to read books worth reading. We vary in age and everything else, but we all have busy lives that are too filled with things that have the words "pre-soak" and "ASAP" in them. We can't waste our precious time reading something that doesn't knock our socks off and make us better people.

The only other book club I've belonged to is the Mother Daughter Book Club in New Jersey. It was a select group, invitation only, and we read the best fifth grade reading level books on the market. I use "we" super loosely. The girls and most of the moms read the best fifth grade reading level books on the market. I scanned the best fifth grade reading level books on the market at red lights on the way to the book club meetings and in the driveway while the other moms were organizing the craft and setting out theme-related refreshments. I wasn't always sure what the theme was, especially if a price tag was covering the description on the back cover.

"You had a whole month to read the book," my daughter would lecture me, as she tied my shoes and reached over to turn on the car ignition while I flipped pages. "Didn't you say last month that you were never going to wait until the last minute again? You'd think that incident where you didn't know the main character's name in *The True Confessions of Charlotte Doyle* would have taught you a lesson, missy. Now just go in there and fake it the best you can, and promise yourself you'll do better next time."

It wasn't my finest hour as a mom.

I'm hoping to do better with this new book club. I'd like to model it after my friend and literature advisor Rick's book club in Chicago. They read classics and anything that doesn't bring out the sarcastic criticism in Rick, who can melt cheese with his opinions.

Back at the turn of the century (I love saying that), I was talking to Rick about the new list that had just come out: the 100 Best Books of the 20th Century. We each got a copy and began going over it. Some of them weren't good enough for him, so we decided to make up our own list. Our summer reading project that year was to make a new list and read as many as we could.

We had a pool back in the late 1900s (love saying that too), so I spent most of my summer lifeguarding my kids and half the neighborhood children fifteen and under; I checked out a stack of books from the library and spent two and a half months reading *The Man in the Iron Mask* while blowing up floaties, *A Light in the Forest* while scooping bugs out of the pool filter, *Sons and Lovers* while giving fake CPR to the seven-year-old drama queen from across the street ("You're fine. Now get back in there and yell 'Marco' louder!"), and a series of 1930s noir detective stories while applying sunscreen to the non-Italian kids. It was a very confusing summer, what with the variety of book genres I was reading and the kids realizing they could do almost anything without me caring, except splash pool water on my book.

Since then, my summer reading projects have not been nearly as focused. One summer I vowed to read *Ulysses*. It turned out the summer lasted seventeen months and, yes, I know it normally doesn't snow in the summer, but that year it did. I went through an Indian summer once and got so depressed with stories about handicapped urchins begging in the streets of Bombay that to this day I can't eat curry with the same zeal. Another summer I got all into the French Revolution and Elizabethan England, and I read too fast and still have a hard time remembering who was burned at the stake and who was beheaded. (Is it "French guillotine and Brits burn"? Or "French burn and Brits guillotine"?)

I'm super psyched about my new book club. I *will* read the books on time. I will *not* wait until the last minute and cram. I will *not* buy or download CliffsNotes. I *will* leave enough time after finishing the book to brush my own teeth before leaving for book club. And I will *not* allow my minor children to run to the liquor store to buy me a bottle of wine to take to the meeting.

I hope I'm successful enough to make it last longer than the summer. The last fall/winter reading project I did was skimming the DVD jacket of *The True Confessions of Charlotte Doyle*.

Hey, Pantyhosers

Pls write about pantyhose.

That message was sent to me by my friend Wendy. It could be a reference to pantyhose crafts (and other tacky '70s handiwork), my sisters' upcoming visit, and my seventh grade brown corduroy jumper. If I didn't mention it, I meant to. There are whole websites devoted to pantyhose crafts. Everything you make from pantyhose looks like a homemade Cabbage Patch doll with cancer who is being treated with steroids and lots and lots of water. I found mention of a book called *More Pantyhose Crafts* on the website Awful Library Books. I think that says it all.

Or it could just be that Wendy wants someone to rip the lid off the pantyhose scam of 1924-2006. I'm just the one to do it.

Pantyhose are becoming today's girdles. I used to look at my mom's girdles with such fascination. Why would someone wear this? Because it makes you look thinner. But, so do enemas, starvation diets, and vertical stripes, but that doesn't mean we should all do those, does it?

Pantyhose don't make you look thinner. They don't make you look prettier. Right now, they make you look like you're living in the Heartland and haven't picked up a *Marie Claire* in a while. They do, however, cover up broken veins, rashes, razor nicks, and other signs of aging and getting-ready-in-a-hurry. Ergo, wearing pantyhose now means you're old, disorganized, and/or square.

I am all of the above. I still wear pantyhose on occasion. When my niece Kim got married a few years ago, I bought a red dress and black shoes, so I got a pair of very sheer black pantyhose to wear with my ensemble. The operative word here is *very*. While getting out of the car to go into the reception, I got a snag that turned into a run that turned into a giant hole. So upon arriving at the reception, I had to skip the receiving line and go directly to the bathroom and take off the pantyhose, throw them in the trash, and go pantyhose-less for the rest of the festivities.

"I was kind of relying on the control top to make me look a little better in this dress," I told my niece Amy, who was in the bathroom stall next to me. I mentioned panty lines.

"That's why you should just wear a thong, Aunt Diane," Amy's bathroom stall said.

Well, way to make me feel super old *now*, Amy.

When my first niece got married, my sisters and I spent some time at the open bar keening about the fact that we were THE AUNTS at a wedding. We are too hip and I, for one, was not busty enough to be THE AUNTS at a wedding.

But then less than ten years later, there I was trying to pull off pantyhose (literally and figuratively) at another niece's wedding.

If the end is near for pantyhose, then we're going to have to come up with something else to filter new men in our lives. Now that the walls seem to be crumbling down, I can reveal that since the early '70s we have used pantyhose to screen prospective boyfriends for long-term use. We did it with a simple request: Could you run into the store and get me some pantyhose?

Seemed easy enough, until he got to the store and saw that the possible combinations of pantyhose are like doing a 3-D mathematical grid puzzle that is only successful if you know every intimate thing about your girl and what she's wearing that night. *Were you paying attention? We'll see. Nude, suntan, taupe, coffee, black, white, or brown sugar? Sheer elegance, ribbed, silky, active support, shimmer, glimmer, or light tights? Sandal foot or reinforced toe? Control top, regular top, sheer-to-waist, or I-have-a-child's-inner-tube-around-my-hips-and-if-you-don't-like-it-you-can-eat-shit-and-die? Size A, B, C, or Q? There is a separate table on the back of the package for size, based on your girl's height and weight. Luckily there are no sizes D through P. Can you handle this? How are you doing?*

He may find the right color and size, with the right toe and the right top, but it's not the ultra-sheer you asked for, but instead the new Body Beautiful Active Smoothers Anti Cellulite, and it's made out of lawn and leaf bags. You *do not* want to take that home to her. Start over.

If your guy comes home wiping away tears and has made several calls to his mom in an effort to get it right, he's a keeper, no matter what he chose. But if he hands you a pair of knee socks, he can hit the road.

I'm Putting the Grr Back in Girdle

I was standing in line at Macy's lingerie department earlier this week, buying a pair of big old pajamas, and something caught my eye on a nearby rack.

It was a girdle. I had heard that girdles had made a comeback, like around ten years ago, but I've been busy. Or I forgot. Or I thought that maybe the term girdle was being used extremely loosely. I thought it was just underwear with a lot of elastic thread running through it.

I had to reach out and fondle this girdle on the rack. *Yep, it's a girdle.*

They can call it a body shaper, Spanx, a control panel, shape-wear, or body magic. You can call it I Can't Believe It's a Girdle. You can put it on a man and call it a mirdle. You can say, "It's not a girdle. I am not wearing a girdle." But, friends, it's a girdle.

The thing at Macy's had a rod running up each side of it, a rod with a circumference of one of those fat pencils they used to hand out in first grade. I now know it's called a "bone." Good grief. Could they make this poor piece of lingerie any less desirable?

Am I supposed to want one? As an over-fifty female who can't figure out how she managed to swallow a fanny pack about two years ago, am I expected to buy one? Most importantly, do I have to feel obligated to wear it and still be able to breathe and swallow solid foods?

The thought of trying to put one on scares me a little bit. I'm not as bendy as I used to be, and I'm afraid I'd get stuck with it halfway on and have to call my husband to extricate me from it. He's a nice guy, but I don't think he'd ever let me forget that. It has Lucy and Desi written all over it.

I thought we were supposed to be happy with our bodies, no matter how saggy, lumpy, puffy, and squishy, and no matter how many fanny packs we'd swallowed.

Bringing back the girdle took a near-miraculous PR campaign. From what I can tell, the message is this: *Phft!* The new girdle isn't for fat people. It's for skinny women who want to look like Joan Crawford.

These are some real quotes from a *New York Observer* story on the new girdle:

"It's for the size 4 who doesn't think she's slim enough or shaped right."

"They're not for hiding fat. They take carbohydrate-deprived, Tae Boed figures and reconfigure them—cinching waists, smoothing thighs, lifting bottoms."

"What you will see is somebody who is fit already, putting on one of these things to maybe enhance a little more."

That settles it: I'm not a size 4, I'm not carbohydrate-deprived, I don't do Tae Bo, and I'm not "fit already." The new girdle is not for me. Bring on the big old pajamas.

Getting Thongs Back on Your Feet Where They Belong

You have to give credit to the guy in charge of marketing the thong. It's a public relations miracle that women are still buying them. I don't know who he is, but I hope he's sitting on an island somewhere being served an umbrella drink by a woman wearing one. He deserves it.

Isn't it time thongs went off quietly into the whorish night? Don't we baby boomers have enough to feel old about without having to see the top strap of a thong every time a salesgirl bends over to find the flannel nightgowns in our size?

And don't even tell me that you're pro-thong because of the panty line argument. We proudly showed our panty lines for all the world to see for thousands of years, but suddenly you wouldn't be caught dead with panty lines? You'd rather wear a slingshot than show evidence of a pair of Hanes for Her?

There are worse things than panty lines. I was in church once, sitting behind a woman wearing a pair of clingy beige dress pants. I pay attention in church (I do), but when I'm listening I sometimes let my gaze drop to what's in front of me. What was in front of me was this woman's behind in the beige pants, and as I stared at it I could see the little pockmarked, dimpled skin often found on the butt. At first I thought she had some kind of textured underwear on, but—no panty lines. She was either wearing no underwear or she was wearing a thong. End result was you could see the rippled skin of her rear. Needless to say, this was a huge distraction from the homily.

The thong marketing guy has convinced a lot of women that it's better to see your bare butt than to see panty lines. He's also making a strong case for thongs being sexy.

I once read a women's magazine columnist who made the case for thongs. Although I can't remember what magazine or why on earth I would be reading such a thing, stranger things have happened at the grocery store checkout. The columnist said something like, "Every woman should have a thong. If you have a man in your life, you've got to have a thong." No qualifiers like "if you're under 200 pounds" or "if you can see your toes" or "if you're still letting the man in your life see you naked with the lights on" or "if you have the discipline to stop yourself from picking at your pants the whole time you're wearing one."

There's a small window for thongs. Too young and it's creepy. Victoria's Secret hasn't started selling Hello Kitty thongs. Yet. Too old and it's creepier.

So if you're twenty to twenty-four and built like a runway model, go ahead, knock yourself out. The rest of us should just be happy with our panty lines.

Dry Hair Solutions

I came freakishly close to spending $39 on a bottle of shampoo yesterday. It would have been a crazy source of angst for me and likely to cause some serious stomach upset. I can't believe how close I came.

It all started when I visited my sister Kathy in Cleveland a couple of weekends ago. I never realized how dry her family's hair is until I got in her shower and started reading the shampoo bottles. She had a dozen or more bottles of shampoo, conditioner, and other hair products in the corner shower shelf that promised to hydrate, moisturize, and nourish my hair. Kathy's family had perfectly nice, moist hair as far as I could tell. I had no idea. I had a dickens of a time picking a shampoo, but I settled on a beautiful lavender bottle of Pureology.

Pureology promised to penetrate my hair fibers so deeply my hair would be moisturized from within, which seems almost wizardly. It also would nourish my hair with soy, oat, and wheat proteins, which sounded delicious. The shampoo guaranteed that my hair color would not fade and would be protected from the sun's harmful UVA and UVB rays. (Possibly UVC too, but I'm not 100 percent sure about that.) All that without using harsh, color-stripping sulfates. It is also salt free—with added rose, peppermint, and green tea just for fun.

How could I not pick Pureology out of the smorgasbord of haircare products in my sister's shower? So I squirted some in my hand and applied. I lathered. I rinsed. I did not repeat. And it's a good thing, because I now know I used up about $4.90 worth of shampoo in that one shower.

I must admit, it was about the loveliest shampoo I had ever used. I even went whole hog and used the Pureology Hydrate conditioner, and I don't even *want* to know how much that cost.

For three mornings I used a rich person's hair products with the wild abandon of a recent lottery winner. I felt like a million bucks. My hair looked great and smelled even better. And though I don't have a problem with dry hair, I'm certain my hair was in no danger of getting dried out, brittle, or flaky.

"It's really expensive," my sister said when I casually mentioned how much I loved her shampoo and was thinking of getting some of my own.

I thought she meant it was more than the $1.79 Suave in the family value size bottle that has been my speed for years.

When we got back home, my daughter was going into CVS and asked me if I needed anything.

"Yeah, check out the price on that Pureology shampoo. If it's not too much, get me a bottle." I told her to call me if she was in doubt about what was too expensive.

"The Pureology shampoo was $39," she told me when she got home. "I figured you wouldn't want it."

She figured right. Who says daughters can't read their mothers' minds by eighteen? There is no way in hell I'd pay $39 for 10.1 ounces of shampoo, even if it does make me feel like the Breck girl on steroids.

It must just be me. I went online to find someone else who is appalled at the price of this shampoo but could only find rave reviews. One site pointed out that "it's 100 percent vegan." Another site identified the signature scent as ylang ylang, bergamot, anise, and patchouli. And, what, ground up diamonds? Shredded pages from an original Gutenberg Bible?

I'd like to publicly apologize to my sister for using up so much of her pricey shampoo. To even the score, when she visits me next, I'll have to take her to The Breakers hotel for Sunday brunch. Because in our guest room shower, there's nothing but Suave.

Masseur Me

Am I the only middle-aged woman in America just now realizing how good it feels to get a backrub from a stranger? I used to say I wasn't the massage type, and I wasn't. I'm still not. But once I realized I wouldn't laugh like a third-grader being tickled—that I just might be a real grownup after all—I had to admit it feels pretty good to have your body kneaded like a ball of dough.

Those of you who know me understand what I'm talking about. When I was getting ready to move from our little New Jersey town, my friends got together to plan a going-away for me, and some of them thought a massage and spa day would be a good gift.

"She won't do it," my friend Jude said. "She won't go."

"Well, maybe she *should* do it," someone else said.

"Yeah, she should do it, but she won't do it." Jude knows me too well.

Instead they bought me a Fitz & Floyd plate, which I loved. It would be five years after the plate broke before I'd get that massage and spa day.

My husband and I were in the unlikely setting of Williamsburg, that crazy colonial adventure village, when we decided to get a couple's massage. I was skeptical since up until we walked into the spa across the street from our hotel everyone—and I mean everyone—was in colonial period dress. I requested a male masseuse because I figured if I have to be worked over by someone from the eighteenth century, I'd rather it be a guy in pedal pushers, a puffy shirt, and a tricorn hat than a woman in a bonnet and a long gingham dress. My husband requested a female. We won't hold that decision against him.

Happily, the massagers were from modern times, so the experience was not kinky in a historical way. My masseur was a very twenty-first-century (or at least late '90s) guy named Joseph who treated me like someone who had survived an airline disaster and was being lured back onto a plane.

"Tell me if the intensity is too much or not enough," he whispered in my ear. Hey, watch it there, Joe. You can squeeze my butt all you want, but when you murmur double entendres into my ear when there's sitar music playing and the smell of lemon verbena in the room, well, my husband is right over there, you know.

Or was he? While my table was squeaking occasionally and Joseph kept asking me for feedback, I wasn't hearing a sound from the next table. *What are they doing over there?* I wondered. With my face down in a hole and the lights turned so low, I couldn't be sure. *Are they even in the room? Did they sneak out for an herbal cigarette?*

The couple's massage idea, while nice, is pretty pointless. It's not like you can carry on a conversation with your spouse during a massage. Occasionally I'd say, "How you doin' over there?" and he'd respond, "Fine." I couldn't really think of any conversation starters that were appropriate for a massage room. My question about the water heater maintenance agreement would have to wait.

Joseph told me to let him know if anything felt particularly good, so when he was working on my right sciatica-ridden hip, I tried to think of a proper way to say, "Oh God! Yes! Deeper! More! Give me more of that, Joe!" So I said, in my best scientist voice, "That feels good."

"Thank you," he murmured. I hadn't meant it as a compliment, but I guess masseurs are people too.

Afterward, when Joseph was walking me to the locker room, he pulled me aside and asked about the bruises on my thighs. No, I don't fear for my safety; no, I'm not being abused or even roughed up. I use my outer thigh to close my desk drawers, so I often have a matched set of bruises on both legs. But thanks for noticing, Joe. Please don't notify the police or women's shelter. My desk drawers would be terribly put out by any false accusations.

I've only had Swedish massages. As tempting as the hot stone massage, shiatsu, reflexology, and aromatherapy massages sound, those straightforward Swedes know a thing or two about getting the job done without a lot of fuss. I would never consider a deep-tissue massage or a sports massage, which sound like trouble. My aforementioned friend Jude once gave me a quick, hard squeeze on the shoulders in her own massage method on my deck, and I thought I was going to lose the use of both my arms. And anything with the word *sport* in it brings up bad, repressed memories from the time I went to a chiropractor—he was the team chiropractor for the San Francisco 49ers—and he convinced me that getting my muscles shocked with electricity would cure my back pain, which ultimately ended up to be gallstones. I haven't trusted anyone associated with football since.

For a late anniversary gift, my husband and I are getting another couple's massage at a local spa. In preparation I looked up some other types of massage to consider trying. There is Ayurvedic Massage, where you get double-teamed by two masseurs working with heated herb oils. (Nice!) With Visceral Manipulation Massage you get your stomach rubbed. (Gross.) There's one where you get massaged by bare feet. (No thanks.) Hilot Massage involves banana leaves and can induce labor. (I'm passing on that one. I can't have a baby right now.) Lomi Lomi Massage was invented in East Futuna, a place I've never heard of, so I'm naturally wary. There is Thai Massage, but I think that's just sex with a prostitute.

We'll probably just go with the Swedish again. In most countries it's referred to as Classic Massage. And for a down-to-earth girl like me, that's about as massagey as I get.

Try This on Your Face

Have you ever been to Sephora or Mac or a department store makeup counter and seen a woman sitting in a highchair getting her makeup done?

What an idiot. Right? I am more envious of the women in line who are buying gratuitously overpriced makeup than the chick who's getting the good stuff put on her face for free. Because in order to get the makeup applied by the expert, you have to do it in front of everyone in your tri-county area.

So of course I did it.

My husband and I were at Sephora (yes, they let him in) to buy our daughter a gift card for Christmas when the makeup saleslady told us that if we bought her a $125 gift card, she would get a free makeup consultation/demonstration/application/makeover for free.

It was a week before Christmas, and my husband possibly had just realized he didn't have a gift for me yet, so he said, "Maybe you would like one of those thingydoodles too."

So I said, yes, sure, I'd love to have a makeup consuldemocation.

The day of my appointment was the same day my husband sliced open his finger on a new knife. I had to race to Sephora from the Urgent Care. During his stitches, whenever I looked at my watch, he would say, "Oh, I'm sorry if my nearly amputated index finger of my right hand—and I'm right-handed—is keeping you from your important appointment. What is it again? Oh, that's right. Getting your *makeup done*." I nearly slipped and fell on the dripping sarcasm.

Other than racing there and starting late, it all went swimmingly. I got over my humiliation of sitting close to the busy checkout line and even snapped a photo of myself with the mud mask on. Or was that the GlamGlow Super Sexy Super Radiant Tingling & Exfoliating Mud Mask ($69)? Yes, I believe it was.

I humbly sat still while my makeup expert told me how I could make my nose look smaller and thinner, my fifty-something crevices look more like forty-something crevices, and how my fear of black mascara is irrational.

"So are you going anywhere special tonight?" she asked as she applied what felt like way too much blush. Or was that too much Nars Glimmer Blush Orgasm Peachy Pink with Shimmer ($28). Yes, I'm sure it was.

I was embarrassed to say I was planning to stay home and watch a Netflix movie about the prickly relationship between Sigmund Freud and Carl Jung and finish off the Williams-Sonoma peppermint bark.

"Well, depending on how I look, I might have to go to dinner. Or something," I said weakly.

I called my husband on the way home from the mall and suggested we go to dinner. Or something. He had sufficiently recovered from the stitches, but the local anesthetic hadn't worn off yet, so he suggested we hurry up and get the first glass of wine in, so as to dovetail on the numbing.

My daughter snapped a picture of us before we left for dinner, and it wasn't until the next day when I saw the photo that I realized I had on way too much makeup. Maybe too much Dr. Jart + Water Fuse Smart Gel BB Ultra Hydrating + Memory Activated Formula ($36) and definitely too much bareMinerals Remix Ready Eyeshadow 4.0 ($30). Also, my fear of black mascara was well founded, as it turns out.

As I looked at my makeup demo face in the mirror, I was grateful I hadn't scheduled a hair appointment on the same day. This kind of makeup might be fine for '70s bands and some other women, but not me. I thought about at least wiping off the lipstick. But it was Buxom Fully Loaded Lip Plumper ($19), and I couldn't afford to waste it.

Seven

Have I Got a Story for You

The King's Inn and He's Kind of a Creeper

When I was young I did a stint as a cook at King's Inn, a restaurant in Lowellville, Ohio, that specialized in fish. If there is a job worse than being a waitress next to an interstate highway in Ohio (my previous job), it's being a short-order cook on the Ohio-Western Pennsylvania border.

I feel comfortable writing candidly about King's Inn because:

a. Most of the people I worked with there have most certainly died of alcohol poisoning, some kind of cancer, or scurvy, since they drank all three meals a day, smoked cigarettes even in their sleep, and had oodles of unprotected sex.

b. The place burned to the ground a couple of years ago, taking with it anything that could contradict my version of it. Although I'd like to point out that I don't make up anything in my stories.

I got the job there the summer after my senior year of high school, a summer I had not planned to work at all since I had sacrificed being in the school musical and other senior year antics because I worked at Al Tell's Pharmacy my senior year. I figured since I had saved up all that money, I could chill out over the summer and start college well rested.

But about a week into the summer, I got second thoughts. All my friends had jobs. My boyfriend had joined the Navy. Was the universe trying to tell me something? It was time for me to go to work, even if it was just for something to do.

My friend Terry told me about King's Inn, just a twenty-minute drive from my house, literally on the border of Ohio and Pennsylvania. It had an Ohio address, but if you walked out the side door of the kitchen and flicked your cigarette butt, it would probably land in Pennsylvania. King's Inn was famous for its fish dinners on Fridays. The fish was haddock and you could get it broiled if you were crazy. If not, you would get it deep-fried. It was served with french fries (or baked or mashed if you were ridiculous), a lemon wedge, and a sprig of parsley. There may have been some coleslaw involved.

It was super delicious. I'm not kidding, I don't think I've had as good a fried fish dinner since.

The place also was a motel, specializing in people having affairs, making the restaurant a good place to get a bite to eat before you got down to business. There was also a bar, which was open until 2:30 a.m. (as per Ohio regulation at that time and probably still), but it opened at 7 a.m.

Terry had worked there as a cook and probably felt guilty that he was blowing that pop stand, so he talked me into applying for a cook's job. I don't think there was an interview. The manager, Gary, was hugely obese and lived in the apartment above the bar and restaurant. He was so large he really didn't go anywhere. I don't believe he had a driver's license or could fit into a car. Someone told me I shouldn't feel bad about Gary not leaving King's Inn proper, because he had prostitutes brought in on a regular basis.

Gary told me he gained weight just by being in a kitchen all the time. There was a lot of grease in there, and he claims that it could get into your body simply by being in the same room. Osmosis or something.

I first worked the dinner shift, which was okay except for Friday nights, when the entire states of Ohio and Pennsylvania would come in for the fish dinners. It was crazy how much fish we fried. Someone's whole job was to go to the refrigerator and roll out huge pallets of fish, then take them over to the cook, who put them in a fryer the size of a hot tub.

When I first got scheduled for the early morning shift, Gary had had way too much to drink the night before, so he slept in and wasn't there to train me on how to cook eggs for the guys in the bar, who showed up at 7:01 a.m. wanting their beer-and-egg breakfasts.

I panicked and went upstairs and banged on Gary's apartment door a couple of times, to no avail. The bar maid took pity on me and came back to the kitchen to help me make some eggs. I had finished with about six orders when Gary finally came stumbling in and raised holy hell because I hadn't used the non-stick egg frying pans properly.

We weren't allowed to use any utensils on the non-stick egg frying pans. Not even soft plastic. So after he yelled at me until I almost cried, he showed me how to flip eggs using just the pan and my limber wrists. It took me about two dozen eggs, but in the end I was able to flip eggs over without breaking them, and without using a spatula. It's a talent I still possess. If you come to my house, I will flip you an over-easy egg and you can thank Gary for it.

My coworkers at King's Inn were great, but keep in mind I was a relatively naïve Hubbard girl, suddenly exposed to people with sordid pasts and weird physical and mental situations.

The people who worked with me in the kitchen were:

- Phyllis, a lady who had had her nose half bitten off by her best friend's dog years before. You could still see the chomp mark and the deep indentations around the circumference of her nose that the dog left. She only had a few teeth too. The thing I remember most about Phyllis is that she blew up a microwave once by putting a potato in there without first forking it.
- Sheila, a girl my age who was married with three little kids. Her husband had recently stabbed someone to death in a bar and was in prison serving a life term. Sheila was poorer than dirt. Phyllis used to give Sheila whole roast beefs and whole hams to take home a couple nights a week. To say there was little to no inventory control was an understatement. We all brought our old clothes in for Sheila to have.

- The three Weber brothers, early pioneers in job sharing. I think their mom got them a couple of collective jobs at a couple of restaurants, and she would just send in some of them to do a shift. You never knew which one was coming in. The schedule would just say Weber. This guaranteed that their shifts never went unfilled because of illness or doctor appointments. There was always another Weber to step in.

Eventually, Gary—who was really a nice guy as it turns out, despite the prostitutes and his obsession over the non-stick pans—left for less greasy pastures. Peg, the bar manager, took over the restaurant, bar, and hotel kit and caboodle, and the place was never really the same. It was run like a real business, which was no fun at all.

The summer I worked at King's Inn I spent most of my spare time there too, in the bar, drinking with the other employees. The waitresses were mostly quasi-young, quasi-single girls. I don't think anyone had any kids or many responsibilities. None of us acted like it. The place could really suck you in, I'm telling you, as we all saw what happened with fat Gary. Sometimes I would go home with one of the waitresses named Sherry (there were two of them and they were best friends), and we would just crash. Before you knew it, it was time to start flipping eggs again and it would start all over.

I was only eighteen, so I guess that was as good a time as any to be involved in the seedy underbelly of Western Pennsylvania.

My friend Barb, who sends me stacks of Hubbard newspapers every few months, included a newspaper story when King's Inn burned down. It was really sad. So many memories, gone.

I scanned the photos of the smoking embers to see if I could see that non-stick pan. If it ended up scratched, it wasn't me.

Fake Kidnapping But Only as a Last Resort

I was reading recently about the boy in Alabama who was so worried about what his parents would think of his report card that he faked his own kidnapping. He showed up at his grandparents' house some time later, claiming to have escaped from the moving car of his kidnapper. Had to leave the backpack and report card behind, dang it! But was able to carry his instrument case with him.

I don't know what he plays, but unless it's the piccolo, there must've been some James Bond moves in that story somewhere. My daughter plays the bassoon, and she can barely get her instrument case between the vehicles in our driveway when walking into the house, let alone out of a kidnapper's moving car. I'm sure his band director was proud of him, screwing up his fake kidnapping story just to live up to the Never Abandon Your Instrument rule.

And how cute is he that he thought his parents might never know what grades he got, because he was kidnapped on the day report cards came out? We tell them over and over about the power of the permanent record, but they just don't listen. Cute little buggers.

The story made me think of a guy I knew in college who faked his own kidnapping to avoid taking a final he hadn't studied for.

When my roommate Doria and I found out about this, we thought it was the funniest thing that had ever landed in our laps. Whenever we would see him, Doria—who could have been a stand-up comedian she's so freaking funny—would put a gun-shaped hand to her own head and whisper, "Come with me and nobody gets hurt." Doria and I got a ton of mileage out of the guy. He seemed to be everywhere we went on campus. And he was dating a girl on our floor (not on our actual *floor*, people . . . it was the crazy '70s and everything you've heard is true, but we did sleep on beds).

The kidnap guy and his girlfriend were one of the more unusual couples in our dorm, and that's saying a lot, believe me. He had the whole fake kidnapping thing attached to him like a barnacle for life, and she was seriously obsessive-compulsive, but this was before we knew it was a medical condition, a real thing with a label and a doctor's excuse. We thought she was just really clean.

She took seven showers a day and washed her hair three times a day. Sometimes more. If she got any dirt on her at all, or sweated, she would throw in a couple extra showers.

She had long straight shiny hair and of course had to blow dry it after every hair washing. We were fascinated, listening to her tell about the showers, which she did gladly for our amusement. The story went something like this: She took a shower when she first woke up, before anything else. Then she'd take another shower and go to breakfast. Then she'd zip back to the dorm and take another shower before her first class. There were more showers in between some classes and then a few more at night. She too was unaware of the OCD thing.

"I'm just really clean," she told us. We agreed and did not call the Help Hotline to tell on her.

I was not without my own weirdness in college. I almost tore out both of my eyebrows worrying about a psych paper I had to write on auditory processing. Let's face it: I was weird. But that did not stop me from ruthlessly making fun of the kidnap guy.

I can honestly say that as unprepared as I was for some finals, I always saved my ace in the hole—the All Nighter—for my get-out-of-fail-free card, and I knew better than to use that up and have nothing left. Nothing but a fake kidnapping, that is.

I never took as much as a NoDoz to stay up late either, and I'm not just saying that because my kids may read this. My roommates—who, once we were out of the dorm and living in large groups in commune-like houses, were a bizarre combination of drop-dead gorgeous professional models, regular people, and one cage dancer—knew what to take to stay up late without putting your heart into arrhythmia. But I just drank coffee, stayed up, and studied my head off. Sometimes Doria would stay up with me, telling me jokes and doing impersonations to keep me alert. I graduated cum laude with no serious addictions other than coffee and got a job in my field, weirdnesses and all.

And as far as the report card years, I did have one bad experience. In the fourth grade, Miss Patrick gave me my first C, and I walked the fifty yards from the school to my house in a trance. I had no feeling in my arms and a cold chill. Looking back now, I'm sure I was in shock and needed to have a warm blanket thrown over me stat. I crossed the street without waiting for the safety patrol guard, and he—a big eighth grader—was yelling at me to stop, but I just kept walking right into my front door. I approached my mother and tried to tell her about the C report card tragedy, but I had held in tears long enough that I suffered that breathing thing where you are spasmodically inhaling in short bursts and you can't talk or exhale properly.

"I *heeee* GOT *heeee* A *heeeee* C *heeeee* ON *heeeeeeeeee* MY *heeee* REPORT *heeee heee* CARD!" I managed to wheeze out.

As stressful as that was, and as trying as college was, I can proudly say that I never considered faking my own kidnapping.

I may have had no eyebrows, but at least I had my dignity.

Esther Hamiltonization

Someone recently brought up the subject of Esther Hamilton, an old reporter for the Youngstown *Vindicator*. I am so glad. I was beginning to think I dreamed her.

But as it turns out, I think she was a real person. For Youngstowners of my generation and the two before it, Esther was legendary. Kind of like King Arthur, where it sounds like it could be true, you're pretty sure it was real, but then you hear the Merlin part and you think, *nah, this is just made up.*

Esther had been a reporter in Youngstown since 1918. By the time I got my journalism degree, more than sixty years later, she was still writing away, her little headshot showing up on her column a couple times a week.

She was Youngstown's own sob sister. She had been one of those newswomen you see in movies from the '30s and '40s, wearing a suit, ankle-strap shoes, and a hat—in fact Esther was somewhat known for her hats. She covered all the big stories of the day, at a time when a medium-sized paper in a medium-sized city would send its own reporters out of town in a big black Studebaker to cover big national stories.

Later she wrote a column called Around Town, where she passed along little tidbits about what was happening in and around Youngstown, with her personal take on things inserted.

Then she got old and moved to Florida, but still continued to write the column. Her column about Youngstown happenings. From Florida.

People would send her notes in the mail about what they were doing, and she would compile it all from her screened lanai and mail it back to Youngstown with her comments. Her commentary was often about how kids today are whippersnappers who show no respect and commit crimes. One time she actually said—and I loosely paraphrase—*All young people today just want to rob 7-Elevens and buy champagne.*

Then she got super old and still continued to send in pieces of paper with writing on them to the *Vindicator*, and the managing editor would rewrite it and run it under Esther's name with a headshot from the 1960s, with cat-eye glasses and a Marcel.

Dan Leone, who writes for the *San Francisco Bay Guardian*, recently mentioned Esther in a column. When he was growing up, he thought it was hilarious and beautiful that Esther would write Around Town "from her retirement home in Florida" and "we'd all trudge through the snow to get the paper and read her." Nice touch, Dan . . . living in California and you had to say something snarky about the snow in northeastern Ohio.

Then she got even older and announced her final retirement. A new reporter who didn't know enough to look busy or be in the bathroom or the morgue was asked to call her in Florida, do an interview with her, and write the retirement story.

I still have the clip somewhere. I'm afraid to read it though, because I think I may have made the whole thing up.

Up until that phone call, my only near encounter with Esther was when she called our house to ask my sister Pam something about the *Vindicator* Spelling Bee and she yelled at Pam, the sweetest and most sensitive of the Laney sisters by far (not to mention the best speller), and hung up on her. Our family was in awe and fear of Esther.

Needless to say I'd rather have crawled on my hands and knees through spilled chemicals on Interstate 80 than call Esther Hamilton at her retirement home in Florida. And that was before I knew Esther was deaf, which made a phone interview seem like a ridiculous idea.

But when managing editor Annie Przelomski came out of her office and walked up to your desk, with that three-foot-long cigarette dangling out of her mouth, and said, "Call this number and interview Esther Hamilton. She's retiring," you picked up the phone and you called Esther Hamilton.

I had to use the office of our former publisher, the late Mr. Brown, because it was one of the few places in the newsroom that had a door you could close. I went behind the big wooden door and called the number; Esther answered and said HELLO!

I said something like, "HELLO! THIS IS DIANE LANEY FITZPATRICK FROM THE VINDICATOR!"

I screamed the entire interview into the phone. Even then, she couldn't hear me and some of her answers didn't quite match up with my carefully—albeit quickly and nervously—crafted questions. She had no idea what I was saying, and I was furiously jotting down stuff that she said.

I kept thinking, *This woman covered the Lindbergh baby kidnapping, for goodness's sake, and I'm talking to her about the Pyatt Street Market? What's wrong with me?*

When I opened the door to Mr. Brown's office, I was sweating profusely and my big '80s hair had gone limp. Everyone was looking at me.

Of course, when she died, the whole Esther file got dumped back onto my desk, and I had the privilege of writing her obituary. By then, though, she had become retro and cool again—getting her out of circulation helped—and I proudly wrote her obit.

Whenever people asked me what I covered at the paper, I would say, "Boardman, obits, and Esther." And everyone got it.

Mit a Side of Dummkopf

Have you ever had to come up with your most embarrassing moment and couldn't think of what it was because you're skilled at blocking out bad memories and you choose to live in a world where you're as refined and smooth as a spokesmodel? Well, here's a tip: Ask your family what it was and they'll come through in spades, bringing out of cold storage everything you've ever done that made them laugh and point their fingers at you.

My family is a walking encyclopedia of every stupid thing I've ever done. I occasionally look for websites called Bonehead Things My Mom Does, because with their combined experience in technology, writing, and Web design, my kids could be making a decent side income on such a site.

They remember every time I mispronounced a word. I won't be writing about any of those because they're only funny if you can hear them being mispronounced. "Merlot." See? Not funny.

Here's the only embarrassing story I can remember on my own:

My husband and I were still in the "lunch-and-other-daylight-activities" phase of our dating relationship. We had gone to lunch twice (Correction: We had had two lunch dates, but he stood me up for the first one—and no, that's not my most embarrassing moment), we had gone to Mill Creek Park, and we had driven up to Kent to pick up my ironing board, which I had left in the house I used to live in. (No, that's not it either.) I think there was a stop at the grocery store as part of that trip, so I could buy some Milk of Magnesia. (No.)

After all that, he asked me to lunch again. He suggested this little German restaurant just off Wick Avenue on the north side of Youngstown.

So we sat down, and I was looking at the menu and recognized some of the German things on the menu, like der wienerschnitzel, der bratwurst, and der sauerkraut. Also der chicken fingers.

The side dishes I was having a little more trouble with. So I asked the waitress, "What's mit?"

"What?" she said.

"What's mit?" I repeated. "I notice that most of these lunch entrees come with something called 'mit.'"

I can't remember if it was the waitress or my husband who told me that "mit" means "with" in German. So "der bratwurst mit sauerkraut" would be only the two things on the plate.

My husband has told that story as recently as six weeks ago. Over the past twenty-seven years, it has been puffed up with embellishments, tinsel, and lights. By the late 1990s, it was an international incident, the entire kitchen staff was involved, and the German embassy was notified, and they are still laughing their arsches off.

I don't know how a person's supposed to forget all the embarrassing things she's done with these constant reminders. It's getting kind of hard to keep up the spokesmodel lifestyle.

My Mom and Willie Nelson

My friend Jackie said recently: "You can't be in a bad mood when listening to Jack Johnson." I gather that she had been having a bad day at work and put in her earphones (the adult version of covering your ears and going "Blah Blah Blah Blah I'm NOT LISTENING!"). And she Jack-Johnsoned herself right into a better mood.

I feel the same way about Willie Nelson.

I had just been thinking that you can't be in a bad mood when listening to Willie Nelson. It was the day I was marveling over my revamped iTunes and playing some new music that someone had given us. I got down to the W's and discovered that my Willie Nelson music collection has grown considerably.

Willie has always been my go-to music when I need to put all my troubles into perspective. It's kind of hard to worry about your kids' grades, retirement savings, or your decision to go with Huntington Beige instead of Monroe Bisque in the back bedrooms when you're listening to a guy who wears the same black T-shirt every day and whose sister brushes out his braids every night in the tour bus.

Suicide prevention counselors should use Willie in cheer-up sessions. Who could contemplate ending it all when you hear "There are worse things than being alone" and "If the world keeps on turning as I'm sure it's bound to do, I'll keep on loving you" and "I gotta get drunk and I sure do dread it, 'cause I know just what I'm gonna do." Perspective, people; ever heard of it?

It's going to be a sad day when Willie Nelson dies.

I know he's human and he has a lifespan of only slightly longer than regular middle-class people. From what I understand, the rich and famous live longer because they have "people to do that" when it comes to stress, driving on the freeway, heavy lifting, and other unhealthy, life-shortening tasks. Although I understand Willie does his own taxes now.

Maybe because Willie and my mom had a moment in 1982, he holds a special place in my heart.

When I was a reporter in Coshocton, Ohio, I got backstage passes for an outdoor concert headlined by Willie Nelson. Picture this concert using these elements: rural BF middle-of-nowhere township, Ohio + beer + the heat of summer + beer + girls with no bras and in some cases no tops at all + beer + country music + pouring rain at the very end + beer.

Yeah, I took my mom to that.

It was memorable on a couple of fronts, but she forgot all about the go-ings-on in the *audience* when she got to meet Willie Nelson. (Sorry but I just had to put "audience" in italics; I don't know what standalone word to use for the group of rednecks with drinking/drug problems that had gathered in that field.)

We got to the concert fairly early, and some other nondescript bands were playing. We were shown to the *backstage* area (a cordoned-off patch of dirt with a fold-up table, a couple of chairs, and a cooler of complimentary beers. An open-air Green Room, as it were).

My mom walked over to a gate near the back of stage left. On the other side of the gate was a field and a dirt road. When she learned that this was where Willie's bus was going to pull up and where he would walk to get on-stage, she planted herself front and center at that gate.

She didn't move to get the complimentary backstage food. She didn't move to get a drink of water, let alone a free beer. I brought her sustenance until others started to gather near the gate, and then I joined her. Over the next few hours, the crowd got larger. There was a little bit of pushing and obnoxious behavior, but my mom stayed put. Smiling, stoic, and front and center of the gate.

Sure enough, after a long time, here came that big black bus with the air-brushed Indian scenes on the side. After a long, long wait, some people started to get out of the bus.

And then here comes Willie, walking straight up to the gate. He saw the crowd waiting for him and smiled and walked up closer. And then he saw my mom. I'm not kidding, his face lit up. He looked like he recognized her. He walked straight up to her with his hands out and took her hands in his and said "Good to see you" or something like that.

I was too busy snapping photos of Willie over my mom's head to register what he actually said. I was stunned by his reaction at seeing my mom, a woman in her late fifties, shorter than anyone else at the gate (and probably at the whole concert for that matter.) But he was genuinely glad to see her.

I heard Michael Keaton tell a similar story about his mom and Pope John Paul II. That His Excellency treated old Mrs. Keaton like she was the most special person in his supremely important life right at the moment. And that forever after, Michael Keaton had a respect for the pope that is unique to people who treat your mom right.

I don't know about the pope, but I think Willie Nelson was glad to see my mom because she was close to his own age, she was dressed like a normal person, and she wasn't blotto drunk in the middle of an August day. Plus my mom always had FRIENDLY LADY written all over her face. Everyone liked her.

So when I hear Willie, I think of him as one of my mom's friends. And cheerful perspective music or not, it's going to be a sad day when he's gone.

Our Summer of the Spider

We technically have a pet again. My daughter just got a fish, so if that counts (and if it doesn't I'm fine with that) then we're officially no longer pet-less.

When my kids were six, two, and an infant, we got our dog Spanky, and I stood in the family room and announced that because we had a dog, we weren't doing any other ancillary pets like lizards or snakes or fish or hamsters or mice and certainly no hermit crabs, those nasty stink-masters. To me, those sub-pets were for families that didn't want to put up with dog hair—animal haters who wanted to get credit for giving their children an acceptable life. No one wants to be the parent who has to explain to the therapist why they wouldn't allow any animals in the house. I was doing the dog thing so I didn't have to put up with all those pet-wannabes.

My family responded to my declaration about the same as they heeded everything else I said: They changed the subject and pretended not to hear.

So over the next years, in addition to Spanky, we had aquatic frogs, fish, turtles, and a snake. We also babysat lots of non-pet pets for other people, including a Komodo dragon, an iguana, a hermit crab that stank up our house to high heaven (dumbest pet ever), exotic fish and I'm sure there were more, but I've blocked it.

And then, when the kids were ten, five, and three, we had a summer with a spider. We foster-parented Legs, a tarantula that was my son's classroom pet. His fourth-grade teacher had a bookshelf full of animals she would send home with students for the summer. Michael came home one day in the spring and said to me, "I want to bring Legs home for the summer. We have to put our names in for which animal we want to bring home, but we need our parents' permission first." He thought he had a pretty good chance because his parents were possibly the only suckers who would allow a giant spider into their homes.

The hardest part of getting the spider into the house was finding the right moment to ask his dad so that he would say yes. At that point, we had been married less than fifteen years, so I was still perfecting the art of judging moods and knowing how to get the desired answer to my questions.

I kept telling Michael to wait. "Trust me, not today." "Still not right. Patience, patience." "No, not now." And then, one morning while my husband was getting ready for work, I went downstairs, found Michael, and said, "Okay, now. Go ask him right now."

Michael stood outside the bathroom door and gave his rehearsed sales pitch, complete with little known facts about the gentleness of tarantulas, myths debunked, and statistics on escapes.

There was a short pause, and then from the other side of the bathroom door he heard: "Okay."

Oh glory, we were getting a tarantula. Mike's excitement was tempered by the fact that he didn't have a chance to use some of his spider FAQs.

Sure enough, no one else in the class got permission to bring Legs home, so he was ours for the summer.

He came with a huge tank or cage or whatever you call those big glass boxes. Inside was a cave, where Legs liked to go to sleep and hang out. We had to buy crickets from the pet store and put them in the tank-cage, and then we'd watch while he ate them. Sometimes, if Legs wasn't very hungry, the crickets would stay around long enough for Michael to become attached to them and give them names. They became sub-sub-pets, which we had to feed bits of lettuce. I waited to find out if we had to feed the lettuce now too. Having a spider was complicated.

Every morning when I went into Michael's room to wake him up, I'd shine a flashlight into the cave and say, "Good morning, Legs." He'd be in there just sitting. Or lying. Or standing. Or whatever tarantulas do.

Then one morning I walked into Michael's room to wake him up, shined a flashlight into the cave, and said, "AGH!" There were two tarantulas in the cave. They were the exact same size and looked like twins.

I thought one of three things had to have happened:

a) Legs had invited a friend for a sleepover and somehow sneaked the new spider into the tank-cage. I looked for signs of a frat party, but other than the fact that all the crickets were gone, no signs of shenanigans.

b) He had given birth to an adult-sized baby. I racked my brain for spider facts about reproduction. Do they have sex? Did he have to sneak a woman in? Is he a she?

c) He was operating a cloning cottage industry in the back of the cave where I couldn't see with the flashlight, and soon my son's room would be swarming with hairy-legged tarantulas that would then take over the world.

I must've stood there with the flashlight, mouth gaping open, for a few minutes before Michael came over and said, "Oh, cool. He must've shed his skin."

Or d) that.

I had to call the Field Museum in Chicago, which we had just visited the weekend prior to see a spider exhibit. I got the spider expert on the phone and he told me how to remove and preserve the spider skin, using salad tongs and astringent face cleanser.

For a long time—long after we returned Legs to his home at Three Oaks Elementary School—we had his molted skin in a jar. After some years, the legs started to fall off and it was just a container of spider pieces. It didn't make the cut on one of our later moves. I think we may have donated it to Goodwill.

My Madcap Summer as a Candy Striper

When I was in seventh grade, my friend Lisa and I were Candy Stripers at North Side Hospital in Youngstown, the same hospital where I was born. In 1971, being a Candy Striper was what preteen girls did in the pre-Title IX era.

We didn't have sports, and we didn't have a lot of afterschool clubs in middle school. An exception was the BBB Club, led by Miss Wire, the most popular teacher in the school. She looked like Miss Alabama USA Barbie. I don't remember what BBB stood for, but I remember that we were supposed to keep it a secret. Looking back, the BBB Club was an all-girl self-esteem club, but they didn't tell us that. They wouldn't tell us what the purpose of the club was, just that all the girls should join. We did exercises and listened to Miss Wire tell us that we were all the *tuffest* in our own way. We went along and didn't bother to stop and think why we belonged. The boys thought we were discussing our periods and called it the Bigger Boobs are Better Club. But that's the seventh grade for you.

So Candy Striping was pretty popular in that it was one of the few options for exploring a future career. If you thought you wanted to be a nurse when you grew up, you became a Candy Striper.

I don't ever remember wanting to be a nurse (sixth through tenth grades were my teacher phase), so I can only imagine that I became a Candy Striper on the urging of Lisa, whose mother was our school nurse and who probably thought nursing was in her future.

We had to go to an official interview and orientation before we were accepted into Candy Striperhood. I don't remember much about the orientation, except that Lisa and I both got very dressed up and also that we couldn't stop laughing. I was sure we were going to be rejected on the immature giggling alone. A dress and patent leather shoes can only take you so far when you're stifling laughter through a demonstration of hospital corners.

But we got the job and started Striping that summer. The most fun I had in the whole operation was getting my uniform and putting in a ten-inch hem, turning it into a mini-smock. I wore it with a white Oxford blouse, white hose, and big rubbery white shoes. The shoes made me feel like a real nurse. The uniform in total made me look like I was trick-or-treating.

Here is a summary of my duties as a Candy Striper:

Passing water – This is not what you think. In Candy Striper/nurse's aid language that's passing out water to all the rooms. We'd fill plastic pitchers with ice water, put them on a wheelie cart, and take them room to room. I couldn't believe how thirsty everyone in the hospital was. It was like an epidemic of dehydration had swept through the place.

Taking poop in Dixie cups down to the lab – The others in the elevator were really mean about it. What was I supposed to do? Take the stairs? They acted like I myself had pooped in a Dixie cup for fun and was riding up and down the elevators just to annoy health professionals. I was just doing my job, people. My unpaid, volunteer seventh-grade job.

Changing sheets – I did learn hospital corners. I even learned how to change a bedsheet with someone still in it. That was a two-Striper-and-an-LPN operation.

Flirting with the cute sick guy – There was a patient named James Long who Lisa and I both had a crush on. We constantly found reasons to go to his room. It never occurred to us that this guy might have some terrible, sad sickness or maybe just had major surgery. We may have been wearing the Candy Striper uniform, but we had not an ounce of compassion for whatever medical malady landed him in the hospital. He didn't look sick at all. He just looked cute.

Feeling sorry for the really sick people – This was the reason I knew at the end of my Candy Striper summer that I could never be a nurse. Whenever I passed water to an old person just lying in a bed with no flowers, never any visitors, I would leave the room and start to cry. That kind of drama was frowned on at the nurse's station.

Lisa and I worked together sometimes. We'd get our assignments—2 East or 4 North—when we got in, and if we were working together we'd be absolutely gleeful. Doubly so, if we were on James Long's floor. I doubt the sanity of the supervisor who put Lisa and me together on a shift. It makes about as much sense as putting two high school buddies in the same unit in a war, or two partners in crime in the same prison cell. It's kind of hard to get anything productive done when you're on an uncontrollable laughing and flirting kick. The patients will get pretty darn thirsty, and their poop isn't going to walk itself down to the lab.

Neither Lisa nor I went into a field even remotely connected with medicine, health, or the human body. I think the James Longs of the world breathed a collective sigh of relief.

Eight

YOUR OPINION COUNTS, BUT NOT AS MUCH AS MINE

This Just In: Suri Has a Boog

I don't think famous people should be allowed to adopt kids. I'm going to go out on a limb here and take it one step further. I don't think they should be allowed to bear children either.

I know we live in a country where we all "have rights." But if I need my doctor's permission to get a refill from 1-800-CONTACTS, there should at least be a form you have to fill out before you're allowed to make new people.

I have suggestions for some of the questions on the form.

- Have you ever starred in a movie, TV show, commercial, or community theater production seen by out-of-towners?
- Do you think the world revolves around you?
- Does someone in your employ do your laundry, take out your garbage, change your sheets, and bring food into your house?
- Is your clothes closet bigger than my 15×15 bedroom? Is there a granite countertop in there?
- Do you think your political views are more interesting and make more sense than mine, even though you don't know what mine are?

If you answer yes to any of the above, I don't think you should have kids. Hollywood people are too self-absorbed to have children. Not that they won't give the kids the attention they deserve, but they'll give them too much attention and bore us to death with the details of the contents of every diaper, every trip to the zoo, and the length of each nap. I think Brad Pitt is as hot as they come, but if I have to see one more picture of him and those six little hippie children I'm going to lose my Fritos and martini lunch.

And the pictures aren't as bad as the interviews. It's only a matter of time before one of them opens his mouth and something like this comes out: "It wasn't until I had the baby that I realized how precious life is. That there's this little person, this tiny, precious little human being who depends on me. I didn't know love until I had Ptolemy."

Really? Huh, funny, because the rest of us think our babies are just little spit-up factories and our lives didn't change at all when we had them. You're the first person to have this epiphany about your values and the meaning of life because you're a parent now. It must be because you're so famous.

There was the time Clay Aiken was all over *People* magazine killing two birds with one stone: My Newborn Baby Changed My Life and, oh, by the by, I'm Gay! Apparently the newborn baby didn't change his life all that much.

People is the absolute best for celebrity babies. It had so many to cover that it started a spinoff magazine called *Celebrity Babies*, because babies are so in right now and they need their own magazine. If you're famous and not able to have a baby of your own, just get on a boat and go adopt one! The black and Asian ones are cuter anyway, and you get double credit for saving a child from a life of having only one bathroom in the house.

Soon *Celebrity Babies* will have to spin off a magazine called *Baby Bump*, because in their quest to be one step ahead of everything, that's what we're now watching for. If you're photographed while shopping on Rodeo Drive and the wind blows your top a little bit, the next thing you know you're in Celebrity Baby Bump Watch with big question marks all around your stomach.

And then in between your complaints about how photographers are always swarming around you, you can tell us how life has new meaning now and having life inside your baby bump is an incredible miracle.

Tell us again about the time you skipped Charlie Sheen's New Year's party just to watch your baby sleep.

Need a Back Rub? Wait Until Monday, Please

I have one more pet peeve to vent about. It's not a super important one because it doesn't come up much anymore, but it used to, and when it did, boy, was I annoyed.

When we lived in Lexington, I noticed a marked increase in the people I saw who rubbed each others' backs in public places. Most often in church.

I'm not a prude, and I'm not against public displays of affection. I think it's sweet to see an older couple or two teenagers holding hands. Or an older person holding a teenager's hand, but only if it's clear they're not dating. And I'm even okay with kissing and making out in public, as long as it's in Italy and the people are very attractive.

But what was happening that bothered me—sickened me almost—was specifically back rubbing.

And I wasn't the only one. My kids memorized the most flagrant back rubbers at our church and would move to another pew if one sat in front of us. My husband threatened to leave the faith altogether by sitting in the front pew. I believe you can be excommunicated by sitting in the front row of a Catholic church, but it would have been worth simmering in purgatory just to not have to watch the weekly Back Rubbers Not-So-Anonymous.

And if you think I'm exaggerating or being too sensitive, or that maybe I wasn't paying attention to the Mass, well, you're wrong. Except for the last part. I actually wasn't paying attention to the Mass because the back rubbing was too distracting. I couldn't take my eyes off the hands and backs, and because I'm just a tiny bit OCD, I would try to pick out patterns in the rub swirls, scratching, and shoulder squeezing.

There were two kinds of rubbings going on, neither of them good. One was the couples: dating couples and married couples, but all heterosexual. Among the younger couples, it was mostly the men rubbing their girlfriends' backs. Back and forth in wide sweeps and then little quick scratches. There is no way it was not irritating to those women, but they never gave him a push or yelled "Knock it off!" or even squirmed in their seats. I tried to stop the rubbing and scratching by boring my eyeball-stare into the scene in front of me, but it never once worked. Not one single time. I don't believe my eyes have any power at all, beyond seeing.

The older couples also included some female back rubbers, who draped their arms across the back of the pew and rubbed their husbands' upper back and shoulders. None of this is the least bit religious, so it should not be happening.

But the couples' back rubbing was not nearly as nauseating as the parent-child back rubbing. It's pretty bad when you are wishing all the curses of Egypt on a mom because she insists on rubbing her eight-year-old son's back during the First Reading.

I have two scenes burned into my brain in permanent ink. One was a woman who came to Christmas Eve Mass and spent the entire service (and it's a long 'un; you Catholics know what I'm talking about) rubbing all three of her children's backs, two at a time, both arms outstretched and alternating among the kids. It was entirely too much movement to be happening in a place with inspiring stained glass. I was so consumed with watching how she managed to keep it fair and equal among the three kids that I heard not one word of the church service. By the consecration I was exhausted, and then she—are you ready for this?—reached up inside the back of her son's polo shirt and rubbed his bare skin for at least three minutes.

"What is the matter with the Catholics in Kentucky?" I whispered to my kids. "If this isn't a sin, then I'm going to have to rethink the whole confession thing kit and caboodle."

The other incident happened at a busy Sunday night Mass. We sat down behind some identified non-back-rubbers, but then they scooted down to make room for a family—Dad, Mom, tiny toddler boy, and elementary-school-age girl.

"Uh oh," I stage whispered to my kids. This mom was a back-rubbing empress if ever I prejudged one. Sure enough, the girl picked up her mom's arm and placed it on her back. That must've been the family signal meaning I Want You to Cross the Line of Decorum and Touch Me Unnecessarily in Church Again. So the rubbing began and continued for a while…until the girl reached around and took her mom's hand, arm draped across her shoulders, and sucked her mother's thumb.

Someone in my family—possibly me—let out a noise.

That was the last straw. Fortunately, we moved out of state and didn't have to choose between going to Mass every Sunday or commandeering the ambo and yelling into the microphone, "You all keep your hands to yourselves!" We all kept an eye out in Florida for flagrant back rubbing, but so far haven't seen it. Praise the Lord.

O Second Cup of Coffee, I Love/Hate You

I have got to stop drinking more than one cup of coffee in the morning.

Ever since I quit my job and became a stay-at-home mom, the second cup has become my downfall.

My life has continually changed since then, but here's a summary of the general sequence of events involving the second cup of coffee:

- *Wake up*
- *Go to kitchen*
- *Make coffee*

I'm leaving out going to the bathroom and stuff like that. You're welcome.

- *Do things like pack lunches, walk a dog, feed a baby, get the paper, convince a toddler to go back to bed, wake up a teenager fifteen times, and other first-thing-in-the-morning tasks that change but reflect wherever I am in life*
- *Pour my first cup of coffee*
- *Drink my first cup of coffee while either reading the paper, checking email, checking Facebook, or reading my hometown newspaper online*

At this point I'm fully awake, thanks to the baby/toddler/teenager/dog and the first cup of coffee, but I'm still completely normal.

- *Pour second cup of coffee*
- *Drink second cup of coffee*

Zing! Pow! Zap!

Holy adenosine receptor, Batman!

I am now a superhero who will organize a charity drive for the kid in the paper who might lose his leg. I will take a bullet for everyone on the editorial page, even the Republicans I didn't like just five minutes ago. And I will clean out all of my kitchen cupboards and put the spices in alphabetical order.

God help me if I've put on iTunes and a song comes on by Melissa Etheridge, Gloria Estefan, or any singer who has ever had cancer or an accident, or any song that I remember from high school. Elton John best stay away from me and my second cup of coffee.

The second cup of coffee has turned me into a sentimental, inspired champion warrior against all that ails the world.

I've learned to stay away from the checkbook at this point in time because I've been known to give away the farm, so to speak.

Before email came to earth, I would just make all kinds of plans about what I was going to do, create lists and charts and go crazy with a couple pieces of graph paper and a pen. Then, when the second cup wore off, I would look at my scribblings and say "What the . . .?" and go back to my regular life—which was full enough without organizing protests and drives and charity balls, thank you very much.

I once read an ad in the classifieds of *The Washington Post* from a woman who said she was a former professional who was now a stay-at-home mom and was bored silly. She wanted to meet with other intelligent women to talk about current events. I was all ready to call her up and start the current events talk, even came up with a few topics, but it was too early in the morning to call, so

I let the idea peter out with the caffeine. I often wonder if she wrote that ad during a second cup of coffee.

But now that I have email and can get messages to the outside world at any time of the day or night, I'm so screwed. If I have volunteered to do something that no one else will do, something that involves making lawn-and-leaf bags full of tossed salad for a spaghetti dinner fundraiser, or anything using the phrase "cleanup committee" or "phone tree," check the time on that email. It was probably during my second cup of coffee.

Experts say the second cup of coffee is when we start to feel the ill effects of too much caffeine: irritability, anxiety, short temper, speeding heart rate, and hormones that turn into a heroin-like substance. Nowhere can I find mention of a coffee property that makes people want to write a book. Yes, I did that too. Woke up one day, drank the first cup of coffee, and thought about doing a load of whites; drank the second cup of coffee and wrote the first twenty-five hundred words of *Home Sweet Homes*.

I've thought about chugging the second cup of coffee and going directly to a third, but I'm afraid the symptoms will double or triple and I'll end up running for public office.

Don't suggest that I stop after one cup. I'd never get anything done.

Adults Behaving Badly

I recently spent four days at a music event for young people and educators. At least that's where I think I was. Based on the behavior of the parents there, I may have been at NASCAR. Or prison visitation.

I've never been to either of those things, but if they're anything like what I imagine them to be, there is a lot of cutting in line, littering, and talking in an outside voice while everyone is trying to listen to classical music.

I was a *chaperon* (not a *chaperone*; my name tag said I was the sophisticated *chaperon*, so I tried to be as French as possible), and I didn't really have any duties at all, so I had a lot of time to observe the other parents. And some of them weren't being very nice.

I'm not one to give daggery looks to people whose toddlers are whining in an audience. It's not like you can help that. Having been there too many times to count (my kids were shy and well behaved until I wished them quiet, and then they were wound-up little chatterboxes armed with fart jokes), I have a lot of sympathy for people sitting in a crowded auditorium with a two-year-old. There aren't enough Cheerios or handheld video games on earth to quiet a kid during a classical music concert, especially during the pianissimo parts.

No, at this music event it wasn't the parents of the little kids who were the nervy ones. It was the people who didn't follow the rules. There are rules. Easy rules. You have to follow the rules.

When the program says No Flash Photography that means you're not supposed to use the flash on your camera. When the program says No Audio Recordings No Video or Still Photography of Any Kind Cameras Will Be Confiscated that means you, big fat guy with the tripod on the balcony whose camera flash blinded me while I tried to watch my daughter play. He must've sneaked out the stage door after the concert. A bunch of us were looking for him.

When the lady comes on stage and welcomes you and tells you to turn off your cell phone, you're supposed to turn off your cell phone. Right then. Right that minute. That's the designated time to check your phone and make sure it's off. The reason she sounds like a jaded, tenured teacher talking to a group of third graders on the day after Halloween is because you all have a bad history of not turning off your cell phones. So she'll be as condescending and patronizing as possible. She may even do a little pantomime of taking a cell phone out of her pocket and turning it off, just in case anyone doesn't understand English or is deaf. Hell, she could put on a one-act play about turning off your cell phone, but she knows, as do we, that someone's Ricky Martin "She Bangs" ringtone is going to go off during the most emotional part of Dvorak's New World Symphony.

When you see an extremely long line that you don't want to wait in, you're supposed to suck it up and go to the end and play with your phone while you wait. Or file your nails. Or put headphones on and listen to some music. What you're not supposed to do is nonchalantly merge into the line six people back. We can see what you're doing. We're not blind. And looking intently at your watch, digging through your purse, and talking on your phone with a furrowed brow doesn't make you look like you're cutting in line unwittingly.

Father Anselmo, a priest at our church in New Jersey, told a story once about how Italians won't wait in line. Italians think that Americans and other rule-following nations are suckers, and they can't figure out why someone would wait in a line when you could just cut to the front and get your ticket. That might be why there are so many fistfights at concerts in Europe. He said he and his fellow Italians from the seminary were going to a concert in London and the line was blocks long. There was hardly any parking. They left their car at the curb and walked directly to the ticket booth. "Damn Italians," someone in line said. Father Anselmo laughed when he told this story. He had not an ounce of regret or shame for his heritage.

Apparently it's not a sin to cut in line. Or to be selfish and boorish and impatient in public. But it does make you look like a seven-year-old to the rest of us.

NIMBY Politics, Literally

The politics of my yard are getting more intense. I hadn't been out there to do a lick of yardwork in a long time, so yesterday I tried to do a little meet-and-greet and solve some problems—you know, let them know I am concerned about their wellbeing and committed to their happiness and success.

The Swoopy Purple Things were not happy about my husband's recent forced eviction of their neighbors, the Rock-Hard Yellow Monster Bush, and they were pretty much staging a lie-in. I had to cut their tops off to get them to sit up straight.

Meanwhile, the Rock-Hard Yellow Monster Bush's replacements were hanging in there. They're a motley crew of ferns, Red Leafy Plants, and nondescript bushes that are happy to be here, but still feeling the sting of the older, more established plants. No one likes to be the new kid.

Getting all the plants, trees, bugs, and other living things to coexist harmoniously is hard work, let me tell you. Someone's always causing trouble or threatening to commit suicide unless we provide more water and food, hire their friends, and clean up the crime in their neighborhood.

The biggest thorn in my side is the Delicate Ball Fringe Weed, which is gaining ground in the front beds. The Delicate Ball Fringe Weed is pretty and feminine. It looks like strands of ball fringe in which the balls were smashed flat and painted sweet pea green. Sure, they look cute, but make no mistake: The Delicate Ball Fringe Weed is the Agent Smith of the front yard. It works undercover and blends in with the bushes you don't ever look too closely at. Then, quickly and quietly, it infiltrates the whole damn bush. By the time you even notice it, it's taken over. You can try pulling it out, but it will break off, thus the *delicate* in its name. And then it will laugh at you and multiply before your very eyes. A lot of my time and efforts are spent trying to save the front bushes from this attractive but cancerous blight.

The ivy surprised us all by running for re-election in the back beds and winning! I thought for sure it would be defeated by the Red Leafy Plants, which ran a tough campaign and got my husband's endorsement. ("We're Prettier and We Don't Want to Take Over the World" was their slogan.) I was campaigning for the ivy but was getting exasperated because it kept overstepping its bounds and climbing up the Red Leafy Plants, threatening to choke them and everything else to death. It's embarrassing when you back a candidate that does something stupid and makes you regret it. But with some help from my clippers, the ivy kept a low enough profile to get another term. Now don't screw it up, guys.

Wisconsinites could take a lesson from the agreement I've hammered out with the snakes. They are allowed to slither and squirm to their hearts' delight behind the row of bushes under the study windows. They could hold satanic rituals back there for all I care. I am not going back there. Ever again. But they need to stay out of the rest of the yard while I'm around. For the most part they comply, but every so often I find a shed snakeskin lying on top of the bushes on the other side of the house. It's their way of saying, "Yeah, I was here. While you sleep, you don't know where I'm going to be. Watch yourself."

We're all about diversity here at my house, so we've introduced plants of all types and colors, native and non-native, ferns to represent the vasculars and spore producers, Those Plants That Start With an H That I Always Want to Call Hacienda or Hyacinth, and even some cacti. Even though we've tried to go all We-Are-the-World and get everyone to intermingle, the succulents only want to grow in their own neighborhood. The two avocado trees are so pissed that we separated them and made them live with others that are not their kind that they both refuse to produce any fruit. "Why can't you all just get along?" I yelled at them yesterday. They didn't answer. They're very good at giving me the cold shoulder.

Sometimes constituents can be such a pain in the ass. Even though I can't remember any of their names, I do sincerely care about them. Sometimes they need so much stroking. At times I am *this* close to bringing in some bamboo just to keep everyone in line.

Nine

My Most Popular Stories Are the Ones Where I Look Most Like an Idiot

What I Know About Fourth Graders Is a Lot

Today was my last day as teacher of CCD for the year. I always get a little sad about saying goodbye to my class. If I were a real teacher and saw the same students five days a week, I'd be a bundle of tears and sobs on the last day. They bring me presents, the girls hug me, and the boys don't trip me and pull my chair out from under me on the last day.

I taught fourth grade this year, my tenth year as a CCD teacher. If you're reading this and don't know what CCD is, it's Catholic Sunday School. CCD does not stand for "chocolate covered doughnuts." It stands for something that I can't keep in my brain for more than three seconds. If I go look it up, I'll forget it by the time I come back here to write it down. It's Catholic Sunday School.

Everything I know about fourth graders I learned in my CCD class.

- No matter what their parents' income, no matter how spoiled they are, when you put food in front of a fourth grader, they will act as if it's their last meal and they've been starving in their basements up to this point. They'll trample each other and step on their best friends' hands and faces to get one Chips Ahoy cookie and a handful of pretzels.

They'll drain a Capri Sun juice box in one cheek-deflating suck, as if they're near death with dehydration.

- CCD class causes staggered bladder weakness. Every child will need to go to the bathroom at a different time, no matter how short the class session.
- No matter what you give them, they'll try to eke out a bit more from you. Pass out a little gift and they'll ask if they can have two. They won't be the least bit upset or disappointed when you say no; in fact they expect it. But they have to try.
- In class discussions, they'll badmouth their brothers and sisters to such an extreme a priest will have to be brought in for a spontaneous confession. They'll tell you they physically harm—sometimes maim—their siblings, and they'll freely admit to lying about them, getting them in trouble, and not giving two hoots about them, as little and innocent as they are. And then they'll ask if they can have a second Tootsie Roll for their little brother.
- Farts don't embarrass them. I think that might start to change in the fifth grade.
- They love gadgets because gadgets allow them to fidget without looking like a delusional psychotic. They'll bring in laser lights, mini-highlighters on a keychain, and anything their parents picked up as a freebie at a fun run. And God forbid they're allowed to have a cell phone. Don't waste your breath telling them to *put that thing away I don't want to see that again if I see it again I'll take it,* because they can't help it. It's a fidget-tool and they've got to use it. In the same vein, it's hopeless to tell them they're not allowed to fiddle around with the things in the Catholic school kids' desks we use. If you don't want the CCD kids playing with your Winnie the Pooh eraser, then I suggest you take it home with you over the weekend. Everything you've heard about "the public school kids" is true.
- They don't forget anything. If you tell them on the first day that you'll be doing a craft with pompom balls sometime during the year, they'll ask you every Sunday for nine months if it's pompom day.

- Fourth graders are the perfect humans. They're old enough to ask interesting questions and understand concepts like how God can be everywhere all the time, how the Immaculate Conception worked, and what it means to covet someone's wife, but they're still innocent and pure enough to ask the big questions. When we had our priest in as a guest speaker, they asked him questions like: "Is it lonely not having a wife?" and "Are you afraid of evil spirits?" I could just cry.

I think "and a child shall lead them" was edited down from "And a child shall lead them. And it shall be a fourth grader. And you shall be amused like the dickens."

Preparing for the Perfect Storm

I'm ready for the big one. Tropical Storm Fay is coming and she's headed for South Florida, specifically right to my backyard, where she will pick up the stone bench that sits next to my pool and throw that thing right at my bedroom window. So says my husband, who dismantled everything weighing more than a palm frond within a mile radius of our house and lined it up in alphabetical order in our garage. The neighbors didn't appreciate us putting *their* stone benches into *our* garage, but, hey, we're new. I think we're going to get away with it. Anything that hasn't been put away as of this morning had to be labeled a lawn weapon and added to my list of things to take care of in the last hours before the storm. So I put *Drag Stone Bench into Kitchen* on my list of storm preparations.

I'm sure we're overreacting by shuttering up our house for what is still a "ragged tropical storm," according to the nicely coiffed weatherman. Fay might even get as far as the Keys, decide to have "just one more" margarita, and stay there for the week. It's not like it hasn't already been done a thousand times.

Besides stripping our neighborhood naked, I did all the other essentials: bought water, bought batteries, put gas in the car, got propane for the grill, charged up the laptop and all the cell phones, and cooked a bunch of chicken.

In my collection of Florida people's suggestions on how to prepare for a hurricane, Mary Ann had a good one: cook a bunch of chicken ahead of time and freeze it in plastic bags. You can thaw it by just taking it out of the fridge and exposing it to the putridly hot, non-air-conditioned house for a few minutes, and eat it. Thus avoiding the canned goods that I forgot to buy.

I have some other good stuff. Like cards and board games, so we have something to do while we're stuck in the house with no electricity. I've got about three hours of battery time on the laptop, and two good bottles of wine. And did I mention the chicken?

Weather is really not my bag, so I'm not going to be your go-to girl when looking for advice on how to handle a storm. My motto on weather-related issues is the same as with most everything else: "How bad could it be?" This makes my husband have several mini strokes in quick succession. Not because he's worried about me. He has a hey-it's-your-life attitude about me, but he's dubbed me responsible for his offspring and his house, so what he's really worried about is the possibility that I'll misplace one or two of them in the midst of a weather disaster because I'm concentrating on a Tetris game.

"Do you have your list?" he asked me as he was packing for a trip out of town, leaving me at home to battle the expected hurricane.

"Yeah, I have a list. Of course I have a list. What do you think, that I wouldn't have a list?" Feigning incredulity isn't really my thing either. He didn't believe me.

"What's on it?"

"What's on it? I'll tell you what's on it. *Drag Stone Bench into Kitchen* is on it. So that's one thing. And then there's . . . um, *Thaw Chicken* . . ."

"No!" He's turning red and looking at his watch. "*Put Up Last Hurricane Shutter, Safeguard Home Insurance Papers, Fill Bathtubs With Water,* and *Get Under Mattress in Closet!*"

Oh, right. That too.

Meanwhile, as I write this, it's 85 and sunny with a nice tropical breeze. Fay is leaving Cuba and headed to Key West for cocktails and a cameo on *Girls Gone Wild*. If I actually do have to go to the mattresses over her, I may do a little bench tossing of my own.

Barney Bean RIP

Here's proof that the Internet is magic. I found Barney Bean on there.

Barney just died this past June. I'm a little upset. Now that all living people can be tracked down and made to be your Facebook friends and get on your Christmas card list, I would have tried to get in touch with him.

The Barney Bean Show was a kids' show on Channel 33 in Youngstown in the '60s. According to Wikipedia, Barney's real name was David William "Bill" Harris, an announcer and station manager for the television station. All I remember are the important things: that Barney Bean was awesome.

If it was your birthday, you could send your name into the show. Barney would sit on a little stool with a giant tablet of paper on an easel and with a fat black marker write your initials really big. Then he would continue to draw stuff around the initials, talking away the whole time. La-dee-da, he just drew away as casually as you please. You'd watch as he drew what appeared to be just a bunch of squiggles and lines that didn't make any sense. And then he'd turn the tablet on its side, and OH MY GOODNESS! It was a cartoon drawing of a face or a funny car with a face or something cool.

Barney had a sidekick, a ventriloquist's puppet named Sherwood, who dressed like a cross between a used car salesman and a Catholic schoolboy, spun his head around, and creeped me out.

I watched *Barney Bean* religiously, along with *Romper Room*—I wonder whatever happened to Miss Rosemary, that Romper-Stomper-Bomper-Booer? And the handful of other children's shows. After *The Barney Bean Show*, Barney co-hosted the *Ronald McDonald Show* with Ronald himself, which was where my favorite TV memory happened.

Every week on the *Ronald McDonald Show*, a different group of school kids would stand on risers, much like a children's choir, but instead of singing, Ronald or Barney would walk around with a microphone and ask some of the kids questions. He would randomly choose a member of the Bluebird troop or Sunday school class and ask, "What's your name?" and then a follow-up question like, "What sports do you like to play?" or "Do you like dolls?" Once, Ronald was doing the interviewing, and one kid in the back row said into the microphone, "Eat it, clown."

Apparently it was live TV because we all saw it, heard it, and witnessed Ronald's shocked expression, even through the over-the-top makeup. We sat speechless on our living room floors while they cut to commercial.

I was young enough that my mom had to explain what had just happened. A bad, bad boy made a joke, and you're not allowed to do that on live Youngstown TV. He got into big trouble.

Then something happened, and like most of my memories of scandals in the '60s and '70s, I've gotten them mixed up with *Law & Order SVU* episodes, and I'm not really sure what happened or what was even accused of having happened. But in my memory, there's a cloud of sadness and pity surrounding Barney Bean and his reputation.

I don't think it had anything to do with the Eat It Clown Incident, but that may have been a prophetic turn in children's TV, the beginning of the end. It would not surprise me to read in a future Wikipedia entry on Children's Television that the death of live kiddie TV was traced back to Eat It Clown on Channel 33 in Youngstown, followed soon by the Screw You Captain Penny Incident and the I'll Give You a Romp Miss Rosemary Remark.

In the late 1970s, when I was a waitress at Howard Johnson's just off Interstate 80 in Liberty Township, I had the counter one morning and who should walk in but Barney Bean. There was no mistake about it, it was him. He sat down, and I poured his coffee and asked, "Aren't you Barney Bean?"

He smiled and said yes, he was Barney Bean. I suppose there's a chance it was a poser, a Barney Bean lookalike who told people he was Barney Bean for the attention. (My cousin Jean worked with a guy who was the spitting image of Sonny Bono, and he used to sign autographs and claim to be him. If you are from Youngstown and you think you got Sony Bono's autograph from a wedding reception banquet hall on Belmont Avenue, sorry.)

My Howard Johnson's Barney Bean took out a job application and sat at the counter filling it out and drinking coffee. I could have wept. Filling out a job application? Barney . . . Barney . . . Barney. Why couldn't your artistic talent and sparkly smile be appreciated and rewarded? I felt so sorry for him I wanted to slip him a free fudge brownie sundae, but he seemed happy enough.

"It's funny to hear these grown-up people say they used to watch me as kids," he said to me before he left.

"Oh, I'm not really grown-up. I'm only twenty and I'm real immature," I said. "I'd watch you today if you were still on."

I'm fifty now (still a little bit immature, but that just means I act like a thirty-five-year-old so it goes largely unnoticed), and I would still watch *Barney Bean* if it were on.

Sherwood can go to the sawdust factory, though.

Neighborhood of Awesomeness

I love my neighborhood. We have a clubhouse divided into three rooms. An exercise room, where I go several mornings a week so I can say "I already go to a gym" whenever a Florida woman tells me I should join her gym and go to a boot camp exercise class. For just four walls and a collection of chrome and rubber, the exercise room takes a big burden off my shoulders, let me tell you. We also have a meeting room where no one ever goes except if you're attending a homeowners' association board meeting, which no one has ever done in the history of the room. And the mailroom.

The mailroom makes me feel old because I didn't think I'd ever live in a place where I'd have to go to a separate room down the street to pick up my mail, at least not this soon. The mailroom is giving me a taste of living in a retirement community, and it's as weird as you imagine it's going to be. I never see our mailman because he puts mail in our boxes behind a wall. I hear him shuffling around back there. It's awkward not to say anything, but it would be even more awkward to speak to him. Not being able to see your own mailman makes you feel like you're a little cog in a large wheel and not like a real homeowner at all.

In the mailroom there are two nice things: a bookshelf where people donate their old books and you can look through and take whatever books you want, and a bulletin board where people in the neighborhood can post things. The bulletin board is like the Wild West of bulletin boards, though, because there are no rules and no sheriff to police it. You can put anything you want up there, and no one is in charge of tearing it down if it's inappropriate or in bad taste.

I suspected there were some neighborhood do-gooders who took it upon themselves to remove things from the bulletin board that they didn't want to see anymore. Maybe because they had been up there too long, or maybe because they didn't want to look at the printout of the big oak entertainment center that someone was trying to sell For A Good Price, or maybe because they thought it was up to them to remove anything tacky. I tested the theory by posting a flier for a group I volunteer for, and the following day just happened to be the day the bulletin board was wiped clean. Coincidence? I don't think so.

So I was thrilled when I saw this notice up on the bulletin board about a month ago:

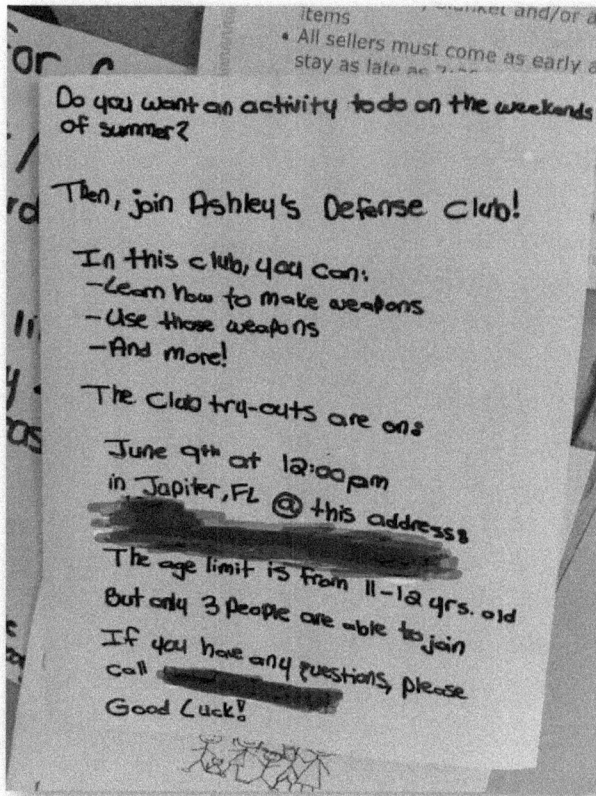

Ashley, I don't know who you are, but you are definitely the coolest eleven- to twelve-year-old in our neighborhood or possibly in any neighborhood ever. A defense club is by far the best idea for a summer project that I've seen yet. I imagine Ashley's mother, on about the second day of summer vacation, told Ashley she should decide to do something with herself for the summer. Something that involves playing with others, building something, and getting the hell out of the house.

Not sure Mom meant that she should teach other eleven- to twelve-year-olds how to make weapons, use those weapons, and more! But that right there is an eleven- to twelve-year-old entrepreneurial spirit.

I like that she is having tryouts and limiting the club to only three people. Make people put a fire under it and join before they can think better of studying weapons training for the summer. It gives it that elite, Navy Seal, Green Beret vibe.

And I love the Good Luck! at the end. Ashley is like the guy on the tape in *Mission Impossible*. Your mission, if you choose to accept it, is to make weapons out of your dad's lawn implements, whatever a $10 gift card to Staples can buy you, and that wrench the plumber left under the sink in your Jack-and-Jill bathroom.

Unfortunately, Ashley's Defense Club flier was taken down by the neighborhood Tight Ass Club the day after it was posted.

I hope Ashley got some response, though. As I drive through the neighborhood, I'm on the lookout for eleven- to twelve-year-old girls sharpening shivs on the clubhouse green. Ashley, if you're out there, I would hire you to build my website or design my backyard landscaping or house-sit or walk my imaginary dog or whatever other tasks I might dream up. The more I think about you, the more I think you're one badass eleven- to twelve-year-old girl who will one day take over the mailroom bulletin board and beyond. Our neighborhood needs more kids like you. And less like your male contemporaries who ding-dong-dash and run their skateboards in front of my car, those futureless D-bags. I will not be surprised at all if one day I'm reading about US President-elect Ashley, who reminisces about the day she formed her first Defense Club.

If My Dog Were a Person

She would be a thumb sucker and have a pacifier and chew gum and chew on her pencils and smoke. And snuff wouldn't surprise me either. She's the most orally fixated dog ever. On walks, she picks up things and rolls them around in her mouth until she sees something more disgusting, and then she makes the switch. Thus, the red Solo cups our neighbors have strewn on their lawn every Sunday morning are regularly picked up and deposited onto the lawn of the elderly couple who go to Mass every day and haven't had a drop to drink out of a party cup ever. Our dog is the great equalizer.

She would be that kid at playgroup who wants to boss everyone around, who you hate out of the gate, but soon warm up to because she has all the good ideas. My dog would be the kid who says "Let's put on a show!" and although she takes the starring role and the tiara, she makes everyone feel so good about their performances that by snack time they all love her and are competing to be her best friend.

She is a party animal—literally—at the dog park. She is the leader of whatever game is being played, but then she takes the time to go to the fence and say an encouraging hello to the little wieners in the small-dog section, who are not having as much fun because they don't have someone like my dog there to lead them.

She would be the president of the Recycling Club and hang posters in the halls, urging the whole school to pick up their cigarette butts. She doesn't like to see trash out in the neighborhood and when on a walk is compelled to rearrange the litter. If there were trash containers on every front lawn, she might actually do some good. She might also take stuff *out* of the trash, but she's still evolving. Maybe she'd be vice president of the Recycling Club for now.

She would be a vegetarian. She gets more excited about finding a mushroom than a live squirrel with an attitude and not enough sense to run when it sees a dog. She's supposed to be a coonhound, but I think if she were hot on the trail of a raccoon and saw a daisy, she would stop and smell the flowers. And then eat them. She has a very sensitive stomach and only feels well when she's on dog food with numerals in the name that has to be special ordered through the vet. The regular meat byproduct dog food with hooves and organ meat, well, that's okay for your dog, but not for my dog.

If she were an actress she would be Reese Witherspoon. If she were an international diplomat, she'd be Shirley Temple Black. She has two moods: cheerful and pumped, and cheerfuller and super pumped. If she were a person she would be in dance *and* soccer. She would have a sensible haircut but sparkly shoes. She would be the person who knows what everyone in the neighborhood is doing and is sympathetic to why they're doing it.

If my dog were a person, she would talk nonstop. She doesn't bark a lot, but she's constantly communicating with other parts of her anatomy—her eyes and ears and tail. Her eyes often say, "Hey! How are you? I'm good. Let's do something. Do you want to do something? I'm up for doing something!"

If my dog were a person, she might be my best—albeit exasperating—friend. But if my dog were a person, then I'd have to find another dog. And I don't think I could replace her.

Dear Thirteen-Year-Old Me, Girlfriend Please

I've reconnected with so many of my childhood hometown friends that I'm constantly reminded of two things:

I look the same as I did when I was in middle school.

I am nothing like I was when I was in middle school.

When I'm forced to think back to 1971, all I can think is *Oh, brother*. And I'm not talking about that brown corduroy jumper. Although that too.

If I could go back and have a little chat with myself as a thirteen-year-old, I would have a lot to say. I wouldn't want to scare her with my neck wrinkles and gray roots, but maybe sit in a dimly lit room and tell her some things.

Hi Diane! And yes, you'll be called Diane. "Di" will never catch on, though you'll have some brief success with "Lady Di" when Prince Charles gets married. Oh yeah! Wait until that happens! She's great, the wedding is magical, and then—um, never mind. Someone in college will call you Dee once and only once. In a rare incident of gumption, you'll muster up the courage to tell him you aren't crazy about being called Dee. Your heart will beat really fast for a few minutes.

Your adult life is really great. Your fantasies of having Ann Stiftinger's haircut and clothes will not happen, but you'll look okay anyway. Your skin is going to go crazy with acne here pretty soon, but don't let it get you down. You'll get modern dermatology's finest, which involves zapping you with cancerous death-rays that won't help at all. You'll follow the anti-acne diet religiously, and you'll go four years without eating chocolate, and that won't help at all either. But when you turn eighteen, your skin will slowly start to clear up. Your face will never win any awards, but eventually you'll be able to afford some of the finest products the makeup industry has to offer, and honey, that's a lot. Wait till you get a load of Sephora at the mall.

Your hair, which Pam has already described as oily enough to make salad dressing, will also settle down. You'll be using Dry Remedy conditioner by the time you're forty.

Those tortoiseshell glasses do make you look sophisticated and beyond-your-years classy. But don't get too attached to them. You'll be glad to know that by the time you put on a wedding gown, you'll have had contacts for a long time. And thirty years after that you'll have something we now call LASIK surgery. Picture McCoy coming out of a Star Trek episode, putting you under a big machine, and zapping your eyes into 20/20 submission. Next year when you read *A Clockwork Orange*, pay close attention to how they hold that guy's eyes open. Never mind. Don't think about that.

Now listen up while I tell you about those popular boys you're obsessed over. They're fine. They'll all turn out to be very nice men, and some will even hit the dance floor at class reunions. (Bring your camera.) But I want you to pay closer attention to the quiet ones, the boys who make you laugh. They'll make the best boyfriends and the best husbands. Not that you'd know that. None of them—popular or not—will ever ask you out. Sorry to be so harsh, but just trying to school you here.

Pay attention in math. I don't care what people say, you will *so* use math again, especially algebra. Don't bother buying encyclopedias or big ol' atlases.

If I told you where you'll get information and how fast you'll get it, your mind would blow up.

Bobby Sherman will stop singing and acting and become an ambulance driver. You will one day tower over Davy Jones. Did the Beatles break up yet? They will. Cat Stevens will grow a crazy-ass beard and change his name to Yusuf Islam. I am not kidding about this. David Cassidy will go Vegas. Oh, sorry: Vegas is Las Vegas, where people go to gamble. You will never go there and you will never want to.

Be nicer to people. You do okay, but you could do better. Speak up and stand up to all that nastiness that descends like a cloud over middle school and high school. If I told you how guilty you'll feel for not being a more honorable person as a young girl, guilt that will follow you into old age and probably to the grave, you wouldn't believe me.

Some people you know now will die. I know you know that people die eventually, but it's really, really hard, especially when you regret not doing or saying things. So just keep that in mind all the time, but try not to let it make you too morose. Okay, then . . .

So let's talk about your career! I don't know how to tell you this, but you will not be a teacher. I know, I know. You've wanted to be a teacher since kindergarten. But when you're a junior in high school, you'll take a journalism class—I can't remember why—and your teacher will be a short spitfire of a woman, Mrs. Alexander. She will make you want to be a newspaper reporter, just so you can show the world what you know about comma conservation.

You won't ever work at the *New York Times*, but the *Niles Times*? Yes, you'll rock that place. It's near the Eastwood Mall. You'll have some other fun jobs too, like making salads and scrubbing pots at the Rathskeller at Kent State, frying fish for drunk people at King's Inn in Lowellville, and waiting on truckers at Howard Johnson's on Belmont Avenue. Those guys *will* ask you out.

And since we're on the subject, you better sit down for this one. You'll be a stay-at-home mom. I know, I know! But when you meet your kids, you'll understand. And you won't ever regret it.

Which is more than I can say for that brown corduroy jumper. And that perm you get in 1985? Girlfriend, please.

Lebron, Dear, We Need to Talk

You don't know me so let me introduce myself. I'm a middle-aged white lady who doesn't know much about sports, but I'm a typical American sports fan in that I'm a middle-aged white lady who doesn't know much about sports.

I don't know a run-and-gun from a Hail Mary—oh, wait, that's football, right?—but I love to watch the Cavs, not because I love the sport of basketball, but because I love to watch *my team* play basketball.

For me it's all about the team. It helps that in basketball you can see the players' faces and body art, expressions of anguish and sweat being flung from their bodies like holy water on a whisk at Easter Mass. It's the most up-close-and-personal sport I know, and that's why I love it.

So when you announced your decision (notice that's a lowercase *d* there, son) to leave The Heat and return to Cleveland, I was not one of the people who said "It's a business decision" or "This is about his career." From my vantage point, you're changing the makeup of my team, so I get to have an opinion.

And I expressed it, badly, by shooting off my mouth before the announcement was even made. The rumors were flying, remember, and all I saw was your face next to the words "What will he do?" and I let my emotions run wild. I called your potential return to the Cavs a "dick move" on Facebook in a post that I fired off in anger. This is something I'm old enough to know not to do, so the post itself was a dick move on my part. But let's not focus on my shortcomings in this whole affair. Let's talk more about yours.

I read your explanation in *Sports Illustrated*, and my sisters are right. You are acting very maturely and seem to have grown up a lot. But understand that when you left Cleveland four years ago, I was extremely pissed off at you. Not because you didn't have the right to go to another team. I left Cleveland too. In 1990. No one seemed to care. I was angry because of what a hotshot you were being. I'm fine with you being a hotshot. But only if you're *our* hotshot.

I was in Paris when you made your capital-D Decision. (And I'm not talking about Paris, Kentucky, although now that we're here, go Cats!) The previous day, I was in the Louvre and saw a big gold tureen with King James engraved on it, and I snapped a photo of it, sure it was a sign that you'd announce you were staying with the Cavs. Although, looking back, that was kind of a stretch. I'm sure someone from Miami was in the museum that day too. The Decision came in the middle of the night Paris time, so bright and early the next morning I knocked on my son's hotel room door, knowing he would have stayed up to get the news. He hadn't even finished opening the door when I caught a glimpse of his face, and I knew.

I won't say it ruined my vacation, but it stained France for me forever.

I know I'm old enough to be your mother's publicist, but we need to sit down with a glass of wine this week. It just so happens that I'm going to be in Akron and Cleveland on Thursday, and although my schedule is tight, I might be able to fit you in late in the day. Leave your posse or whoever's giving you career advice at home. I might bring my sisters, but one of them may have to work, so it could be just you and me.

I'd like to reach some kind of understanding where you say you're very sorry and I say that I forgive you and you say you never should have left and I say I never should have said I wouldn't watch the Cavs anymore if you came back. And then you go, well, we all make mistakes. And then I go, yes, but some mistakes impact other people's lives and TV watching habits in the winter months, which are kind of important. And then you're all, but I'm just a young kid. Didn't you make mistakes when you were in college? And I'm like, yes, but mine was a *real* college and it was the '70s.

And then we can hug and shake hands or whatever and go back to doing what we do best. Kicking the Marlins' asses. Wait, that's baseball, isn't it?

Ten

MY FAVORITE STORIES ARE ALSO THE ONES WHERE I LOOK MOST LIKE AN IDIOT

Antibacterial Soap Operas

was flipping through the channels yesterday and—did you know that soap operas are still on TV? I'm a bit surprised. I thought the *Soap Opera Digests* I saw in the grocery checkout line were antique collectibles.

I found two soaps on at 1 p.m. and both were in the midst of hospital scenes. In true soap fashion, one hospital room scene had a bride, dressed in a long traditional white gown and veil, in a hospital room crying over someone who had just died, and I don't think it was the groom. The second scene had a guy with Fabio hair and an eye patch. Isn't it nice to know some things never change?

Soap operas have really dug in their heels on that working formula.

I watched *The Secret Storm* and *The Edge of Night* with my sisters briefly in the 1960s. This is where I learned that women with the name Margo are as glamorous as you would think. Then the summer after my brother got married, I practically lived at his house and watched *All My Children* with my new sister-in-law. During commercials she would fill me in on the backstories. It took us until mid-August to get caught up, and that was just the stories about Nick, Joe, Phoebe, and the girl who was in *Saturday Night Fever*.

In college, my roommates and I jumped on the careening, out-of-control bandwagon that was *General Hospital*. We used to tear out of our last class to get home to watch what Luke and Laura were up to. We scheduled extra time to hate the Quartermaines and Laura's twerpy little sister, Amy Vining.

In addition to your run-of-the-mill affairs, illegitimate children, and amnesia, GH offered up rape, murder, evil twins, and a gay aerobics instructor in short-shorts. I think this was also the beginning of soap characters having first names of states and geological formations.

The problem with having to be home and in front of the TV by 3 p.m. is that sometimes you were early, so you'd catch the tail-end of the soap before it. It would only take a few days before you'd be sneaking home at 2:30 to catch the last half of that show. Soon you're convincing yourself that afternoon classes are stupid and an associate's degree is nothing to sneeze at. And who really needs a minor?

I heard later that soaps eventually introduced aliens and Satan into their casts and storylines. But there were still hospitals full of doctors and nurses who were so not dedicated to their jobs that they had time to stop and have coffee with Dakota or Siobhan, Ridge or Skye, Calliope or Snapper on their way into the hospital. It's full daylight, so I can only imagine it's about nine or ten o'clock in the morning and they're all sitting around discussing Sierra's birth mother's mysterious arrival in Llanview.

"Who's working the seven-to-seven shift? And why is no one dispensing meds or emptying bed pans?" you want to shout at the screen. I'm pretty sure a public hospital has a gall bladder or two that needs to be removed. And there's the amnesia victim that needs some follow-up.

I'm starting to wonder if they were real doctors at all. Who would let a guy with feathered hair and one eye operate on the love child of the hospital administrator?

An Open Letter to You College Brochure Sender-Outers

TO: All US colleges and universities, private, public, and in between
FROM: Mom of a high school junior

Dear sirs,

What is the matter with you? What are you people doing over there?

My son, who is ending his junior year of high school, is receiving letters, brochures, and booklets from you people daily. Some of them are so big and three-dimensional they come in actual boxes. Some include pictures of supermodel college students lounging on campus grassy knolls, and these photographs are better quality than the exhibits at the MoMA.

We're mixing signals here.

I pick up *Time* magazine, my local paper, or any other publication and all I hear is how hard it is for the average high school student to get into college these days. Did I say average? I mean above average, with an SAT score of 2300, a GPA of 4.1, and a class rank of 90th percentile.

"Phphhhh!" the articles say. "Colleges are becoming pickier. You can't get into even a public university without AP credits, a resume filled with community service and internships, recommendations from professors you haven't met yet, and a runner-up spot on *Teen Jeopardy*."

"But wait a sec," I say. "My son is smart, does well in school, participates in athletics, and can get up and tell jokes at a banquet. He's passed the CATs, the DOGs, and the track team drug test. He'd be a fine asset to any university."

"Community college would be good for him," the articles respond. "Or the Duke wait list."

Then why is he being courted by every higher learning institution on earth? According to my calculations, colleges are spending a very large sum producing these materials and mailing them out to pretty much every sixteen- to seventeen-year-old American.

Here's me, going out to the mailbox. I have to take the Little Tykes wheelbarrow to carry back my son's mail, which is asking—no, begging, luring, and enticing—him to consider going to Harvard, Yale, Boston College, Vanderbilt, Notre Dame, and the Ohio Clown College.

They all seem confident that he is a perfect fit for each of these schools, from Princeton to Bob Jones University. They stress that they're sure he would love it there and succeed like no high school student has ever succeeded before.

Do they know my son?

He wants to major in journalism and he gets invitations to teachers' colleges, engineering schools, trade schools, and Marine training programs. He's Catholic and he gets ads for fundamentalist Bible colleges in Arkansas where they handle snakes. He's a boy and he's been invited to Wellesley College. The letters that accompany the booklets tell him personally that they'd be honored to have him.

They're making it tough on us parents, who are spending our afterschool hours convincing our kids they need to study harder, do the extra-credit project, and kiss their teachers' butts just to get into a school with a dorm and more than one entree in the cafeteria.

"If you want to ever get out of this house, you better study that German vocab one more time, buddy!"

He looks up from his stack of mail from that day and smirks. "According to David Skorton, president of Cornell University, I'm just the kind of achievement-oriented high school student that would be an asset to Cornell's longstanding tradition of excellence."

Fine, go with that, I tell him. But when you spend a semester of tuition money on application fees to schools that won't accept you, maybe Dr. Skorton will help out with some book money at Florida State.

Sincerely,
Bitter and Been There Mom

Why Obama Is Bad News for Dads and Husbands

Attention all American men: The jig is up. We're onto you. We know you're capable of doing much more than you've been doing for the past seven hundred years. We're sick of your whining about having to work *and* change the baby's diaper, work *and* grill up a couple of burgers on a weekend, work *and* go to your mother-in-law's seventieth birthday party. In a clean shirt. We know you can do it, so stop lying.

This illumination is all due to our new role model, Barack Obama, who has invented the New American Male: the multitasking, good lookin' man. This guy represents All That You Can Be to blacks, whites, half-blacks, half-whites, Hawaiians, children of single moms, senators, *Harvard Law Review* editors, tall people, Camel Lights smokers, people who have appeared dancing on *Ellen*, and—the largest demographic of all—men.

It's a lot of weight to carry on one set of shoulders, but he seems not only to be doing it, but giving all you guys a *nyah, nyah* in his spare time, while attending his daughter's parent-teacher conference and fighting crime. I'm surprised he got a single vote from a Y chromosome. He's kicking the shit out of you guys.

Here's just a small list of the claims you can't make anymore now that Barack Obama started showing how it's done:

1. Not being able to wear your good suit anymore because you've been eating too much starchy banquet food "for work" and don't have time to lose any weight. Barack is not too busy to look suave and dapper at all hours of the day and night.

2. Having a job that is so unbelievably important that no one else can go to that meeting set in stone by a secretary who makes one-fifth of what you make, causing you to miss every single piano recital and strings concert for twelve years. Barack doesn't let any underling tell him what his priorities are, and his underlings are pretty much everyone in the free world.

3. Having that low self-esteem that goes all the way back to Eve harping at Adam to "just take a bite and shut up already" and not wanting to fawn over your wife and make her look better than you. If Barack looks at Michelle with any more love in his eyes, her clothes are going to fall off.

4. Not being able to go to the kids' soccer games because "it's not like they're going to be professional soccer players or anything." Barack stands on the sidelines with the other parents and only yells encouraging things like "Go Sasha! Come on, Malia, you can do it, sweetheart!" No damns, shits, or hells, no wife-beater T-shirts with liquor logos on them, and no smoking. And he leaves his iPhone in the car.

5. Not having the energy to go to New York and take your wife to a Broadway play on a Friday night. Barack's day was pretty busy too, I think, and he managed to take Michelle to dinner and a play she wanted to see. It was on his list of Things to Do Friday right under "Pick a lane on Keystone" and "Decide what to do about Putin."

I bet this guy even orders the Saturday movie night pizza, puts away the cereal box when he's done with it, and returns the toilet seat to a more unisex-friendly position.

Is this guy Mr. Perfect or what?

From this point on, single guys are going to have to be a lot more like Barack Obama if they want to play the field at all. We know there are more like him out there, and we're not going to stop looking until we find them all, tag them, and get them married to all the nice girls.

As for the rest of you, you're going to have to work a little bit harder to be more like Barack.

Can you have a high-profile job and still cast admiring glances at your wife out in public, even when she really should not have worn that belt up so high?

Can you find thirty minutes four days a week to go to the gym and work out without boring us to tears with how bad your calves hurt and how thirsty you are?

Can you remember what grades your children are in and which direction the pickup line at school goes?

Can you read a bedtime story to your kids that isn't *The Modern Fundamentals of Golf?*

Can you be more like Barack Obama?

Yes, you can.

Road Trip Food for Thought

I went on another road trip last weekend and spent a lot of time in the car, so just like professional comedians who overuse their experiences on airplanes because that's how they spend the majority of their time, a housewife blogger will tell you all about her car trip to Tallahassee.

The trip was for my son to see Florida State University, although the whole scheme was ill advised, since it wasn't until we got all the way up there that we realized FSU doesn't have a journalism program, which is what he's majoring in. Oops. Which parent dropped the ball on this one?

But that's okay, FSU is still a possibility. He could just major in communications and wing it. If every other college graduate in the last five years is any indicator, he's going to end up working part-time at the mall anyway, so what's the diff? We also got to see the Florida Panhandle. We were almost in Alabama and halfway to New Orleans. The weather in Tallahassee is way different from here in South Florida. It was actually cold. Jack could see his breath when he ran Sunday morning, and he almost didn't recognize it, he hadn't seen it in so long.

But back to the real story here. The trip food. Whenever I'm on a car trip longer than about two hours, I have to build the whole trip around the food, how I'll eat it, when I'll eat it, and how I can make it turn the trip to the intersection of Borestown and Falling-Asleep-at-the-Wheelvania into something to look forward to. I start out every trip determined not to ruin it by making myself sick with junk food. I make lists of bananas, apple slices, pretzels, water, and granola bars. These planned snacks are so healthy I could run a half marathon upon arriving at my destination.

For the FSU trip, I systematically divided the trip into two three-hour blocks. The first block I planned to have an extra-large coffee from home, a peanut butter and jelly sandwich, Goldfish crackers, and, if I got desperate, Mint Milano cookies. My son and his sister went into a car-induced iPod dormancy, so I pretty much had the family-sized jug of Goldfish crackers and all sixteen Mint Milanos to myself. The problem was I got a little bit excited before we were even outside Palm Beach County. I drank the whole coffee and was halfway through my PB&J before I remembered to pace myself.

So at a gasoline stop at the three-hour mark, when I moved into my second three-hour block as planned, I was hungry because of all the caffeine, but at the same time half sick from eating all the Mint Milanos on the Florida Turnpike. When picking out the junk food at the gas station for Stage 2, I did what I always do—I got the wrong thing.

My son says I'm worse than a three-year-old, and he's right. I spend much too long picking out my treats and then have an immediate buyer's remorse and am furious at myself for picking the garlic chive sour cream snack crackers when I was craving something sweet. It has something to do with the euphoria of being outside the car, making me forget what hellish claustrophobia I'll feel once I get back on the freeway, where the snack I picked takes on epic importance.

This time, determined not to be three but having given up on healthiness, I went with my gut craving and bought two Skor bars. By the time we pulled into the Days Inn parking lot Sunday night, I had eaten both of them and the remaining Goldfish crackers. I could barely stomach the thought of going to dinner.

For the trip home, I gave up all hope of being able to fit into my trip pants and not getting a bladder infection. I took two big cookies from the all-you-can-stuff-in-your-backpack Hogwarts Dining Hall at FSU and had those, a bag of Combos, and a super mega hazelnut coffee on the way home. At the three-hour mark, I bought a ninety-nine-cent bag of chili cheese Fritos, a Hershey bar, and another coffee. If there had been pork rinds or heroin, I probably would have bought them too. I had totally given up and was just trying to survive the next few hours to get myself and the kids home. I didn't care if I spent the next two days in the bathroom, I just had to feed my face with something with enough flavor to keep me from losing my mind.

"DOES ANYONE WANT TO PLAY THE INITIAL GAME?" I yelled at the kids thirty miles from home. They squinted at me and adjusted their ear phones. I don't think they recognized me. I had gained fifteen pounds, had bloodshot eyes, and my face was broken out.

My son is making noise about possibly applying to Texas A&M, where I hear they actually do have a journalism program. I'm sending him with my husband on an airplane. My health insurance can't handle another road trip this year.

The Role of the Secretary Will Be Played by . . .

I was having a conversation with someone from my hometown, and we were talking about a family we both know well. He suggested that if a movie were made of this family, Bea Arthur could play the mom. I immediately cast the rest of the movie. The Dad—Scott Glenn of *Backdraft* fame, slightly craggy with expressive eyebrows and a voice like the guy on the beef commercials. The Son—John Schneider with wire-frames. The Daughters—Sandra Bullock, the blonde funny girl from *Scrubs*, and Drew Barrymore. The Dog—played by any small black dog from the pound.

Have you ever cast yourself in a movie? I have, many times. The fact that I've gone from Twiggy to Ann-Margret to Kate Jackson to Diane Keaton to Estelle Getty tells you how long I've been planning the movie version of my life.

I get this from my family. When I told my sister Kathy I was thinking about writing a book, the first words out of her mouth were, "Oooh! If they make a movie out of it, can I be played by Gwyneth Paltrow? . . . [Short pause] . . . Oh, okay, fine. I'll be Kathy Bates."

My sisters and I have cast other great movies too. Some stories just need to be on the big screen, even if that screen is only inside a couple of sisters' heads. A few years ago we took a story that my mother-in-law told me about her friend's aunt in Seattle and how she became a doctor's wife and made an entire screenplay out of it.

The aunt in Seattle was about a hundred years old when she told her niece the story of how she met her husband. She was the doctor's secretary and got to be friends with him and his wife. They often did things together on weekends, including taking boat rides on a huge lake. At the time I heard this story, I wasn't even sure if there was a big lake in Washington State near Seattle. I think it was a rowboat. At least that's how it's going to be in my movie. A rowboat; a young doctor played by Aidan Quinn, with a white shirt, sleeves rolled up, suspenders; the wife, a little bit frumpy without makeup, played by Frances McDormand; and a pretty secretary, played by Charlize Theron, wearing a hat and a flapper-like, flimsy dress. The wife is wearing a hat too, but on her it just looks dowdy. The doctor is rowing, and the ladies are just being glamorous and frumpy, respectively.

According to the aunt/Charlize/pretty secretary, one Sunday they rowed out to an island on the lake, and when they rowed back, the wife wasn't with them. Like many one-hundred-year-old people who were around in the '20s and '30s, she was very matter-of-fact, unapologetic, and not very forthcoming about the reason. "The wife didn't come back from the rowboat trip, so the doctor and I got married. End of story, who wants another cup of tea?"

"They killed her!" my oldest son blurted when he heard this story.

"Well, maybe they didn't kill her," I said. "Maybe she accidentally drowned or just got lost. Or maybe she didn't make it back to the boat by the time the doctor said everyone had to be back or he'd leave."

I could just hear him: "You go off and look for rocks on the other side of the island, and gauze-wearing Charlize Theron and I will be behind these trees in this secluded wooded area with a great view. But be back by four o'clock or I swear to God, Frances, we're leaving without you. This boat is pulling out at four—ass in seat—and I'm not kidding."

If that's true, that's almost more cruel than if they had knocked her silly with an oar and drowned her. Who knows what would happen if she was abandoned on an island for any length of time? How many people got row-boats and went out there? How could she get help? She'd be like Tom Hanks in *Castaway*, pulling her own teeth and chatting up a volleyball.

Okay, I just looked at a map of Seattle and there is water everywhere! And islands out the wazoo. There are lakes and bays and sounds and inland waterways in every direction. Most of the islands are pretty big, though. Maybe Frances McDormand found civilization and started a new life there, working with lepers or retarded children or Canadian immigrants. (In this part of the movie, Billy Bob Thornton and John Lithgow play somebody.)

I'm not really sure any of this actually happened. For all I know, Aidan Quinn just divorced Frances McDormand in a regular 1930s divorce proceeding, which, while rare, did happen. You didn't have to croak your wife just to marry your secretary, even in those more primitive, dramatic times.

But something about it rings true. Maybe because old people have a tendency to look at their sordid pasts with cloudy, glaucoma-gunky eyes and start admitting to having done things, and they just don't care what you think about it. Babies born out of wedlock . . . murders . . . missing spouses . . . My aunt told us that she and my mom used to go to the train station in Pittsburgh and kiss guys who were leaving for the war. Just like a thing to do on a Friday night. That doesn't compare to holding your wife's head under water in Puget Sound, but if we make a movie of my mom's life, it'll have to be augmented with quite a bit more drama.

And I get to be played by Diane Lane.

Now That's Just Adorable

We've been having this long, ongoing discussion in my family—for about three months now—about the use of the word *adorable*.

It's not an argument really, but we all have lots of opinions about adorable and how it's used, who's allowed to use it, and what conclusions you can draw about people who shouldn't use it but do anyway.

We haven't made any final decision about adorable yet, thus the ongoing nature of the discussion. Sometimes we talk about it at dinner, sometimes we mute the TV and pick up the thread for a commercial break, and sometimes we ask that everyone take out their earphones in the car so we can talk about it some more.

My son is of the rock-solid opinion that men should never call something adorable in any circumstances for any reason, no matter who they're talking to or about, and no matter how undeniably adorable the thing actually is.

I think it's a bit more complicated than that. Plus, I've grown accustomed to finding exceptions to my son's edicts. He has equally unyielding opinions on what should be considered a sport. If you think it's weird that we've had an ongoing discussion about adorable for three months, try three *years* on the What Is a Sport discussion.

I believe some things are simply adorable and if you want to make that observation, you're going to have to use the word or be misconstrued. Like the

Eskimos have thirty different words for snow, we have many different words for cute, and adorable is one of them. If someone is adorable and you decide to call her cute or sweet or precious or darling, you're not going to be correct.

When something or someone is adorable, it means that cuteness has gone one step further in a specific direction. For example:

- Kittens are cute. A wet kitten with a tilted head is adorable.
- A six-year-old girl with her front teeth missing is cute. A six-year-old girl with her front teeth missing and a Kool-Aid mustache is adorable.
- All babies are adorable, even the unattractive ones. The babiness alone gets it there.
- A black-and-white photo of a little boy in the 1950s with a cowboy hat on standing in front of a Christmas tree is cute. A black-and-white photo of a little boy in the 1950s with a cowboy hat on standing in front of a Christmas tree crying his head off is adorable.

During one of our discussions I told the story about the time I got a creepy note from a maybe-would-be-stalker when we lived in Virginia. The fact that the note said I was adorable led my husband and our friend Ijaz to conclude that the stalker was a woman, even though the note specifically said he was a 6-foot-1, 185-pound man with blond hair and brown eyes.

"A man would not say you were adorable," my husband said. We were sitting around our kitchen table going over the note and trying to decide who on earth would put it on my car windshield while I was in the grocery store, and what we should do about it. My husband wanted to throw it away and forget about it, quickly, before it went to my head. Ijaz wanted to look up the phone number in the Haines reverse directory and find out who it was. I wanted to start wearing makeup when I ran into the grocery store, because I looked like shit the day I got that note, and now I realized that people were actually seeing me when I ran in to grab some diapers and wine real fast. Sure, the people who were seeing me were creepy note-writing, rapey, kidnappy stalkers, but still. You always want to look good.

The day I got the note, I was driving our Jeep and had my two kids with me, five-years-old and a baby. (Now that I think of it, maybe the note was for the baby . . .) I was wearing sweats, I was still carrying about half the thirty pounds I had gained while pregnant, my hair was greasy, I was wearing my glasses, and I had no makeup on. I'm pretty sure there were no accessories going on either, other than the Michelangelo Ninja Turtle bracelet my son had made me.

I parked the Jeep, got the kids out, went into the store, bought a couple of things, and came out, put the kids in the Jeep, and saw a note on the windshield. I thought somebody had crashed into my Jeep and left a note, so the first thing I did was run around the Jeep in a stealthy manner, looking for dents. Then I picked up the note. "You're adorable!" it said. It also described the writer and included a phone number.

Are you kidding me? I could barely get my eyes off the word adorable. I was just about the least adorable thing in Fairfax County at that moment. I was light years away from adorable. If adorable had been anywhere in my town that day, it would have gone to everyone else's house before it came to mine. And if I had started out close to adorable, my little laps around the Jeep pretty much sealed the deal. It's not improbable that I picked my nose too.

During our most recent discussion, my kids—all grown up now and with no recollection of how truly bad I looked back when I was a novice stay-at-home mom with babies and toddlers—could not believe I had such a note on my car at all. Man or woman, with permission to use adorable or not, they just can't see their mom as the stalkable type.

Someone did suggest that I should have taken Ijaz's advice and looked up the phone number, if for no other reason than to get a hold of the guy and tell him he's seriously abusing the language.

What If My My My My My Boogie Shoes Are White and It's After Labor Day?

I love the new Tide commercial with the sassy black girl and her in-your-face attitude about wearing white pants after Labor Day. "I'll rock white jeans whenever I want to," she says.

Good for you, I say to her. I wish I had half the self-esteem that girl has. I can't do it. I can't wear white from the waist down after Labor Day.

It doesn't matter that I have at least four reasons why I can and should wear white after Labor Day.

1. That girl in the aforementioned Tide commercial. She looks adorable in those stark white jeans, a blue jean jacket, and a scarf around her neck in what is clearly a public park in late September.

2. I live in Florida, where the No White After Labor Day rule is rumored not to apply. "It's Florida!" people say whenever you recite any fashion rule at all. The Florida Rule states that virtually anything goes, and that includes Speedos and bikinis for old people, Hawaiian shirts to black tie dinners, and flip flops to your own wedding. You know how when you were in high school you would hear legend of a school that somebody's cousin went to that didn't have a dress code and it seemed like state-sponsored chaos? Crazy wonderful but scary chaos? That's Florida.

3. The invention of winter white in the early '80s. It was ecru, but who's counting? The point is, people started to wear winter white wool pants and eggshell shoes (with off-white hose, of course), and it was a pretty good look as long as you stuck with the theme. You had to wear a cream sweater with some fuzzy stuff on it, and pink nail polish or the whole look was ruined. Stick a black belt on those winter white pants and you're just another rule-breaking loser.

4. Because I'm fifty-something now, I don't give a crap about much of anything along the lines of rules: I'm not looking for a husband, I'm not going to be discovered by a modeling scout even for the "husky older girls" catalogs. And *Glamour* and *Mademoiselle* magazines don't have a "Do's and Don'ts" column anymore, so I'm not worried about seeing myself on those pages with a big black bar covering my eyes.

I mean, really, who cares if I commit some age-old fashion faux pas? Will I lose friends? Will I miss out on a job opportunity? Will my garbage men refuse to pick up my haphazardly sorted recycling? Will the Bed Bath & Beyond cashier start enforcing expiration dates on my 20 percent off coupons? Because those are pretty much the big-ticket items in my day-to-day life.

So why can't I do it?

Because of my mom, of course. Don't act surprised. It's always the mother's fault.

My mom lived by that rule and passed it along to me and my sisters, possibly through the umbilical cord or breast milk, because it's pretty deeply ingrained in me.

Last Tuesday morning, I went into my closet and grabbed my Florida housewife's uniform—white capri pants, a sleeveless top, and white sandals—before I realized that Labor Day had come and gone; I couldn't do it. My wardrobe for the next eight months instantly shrank, even though the weather here is still 1,000 degrees Fahrenheit with 200 percent humidity. I could wear a bathing suit, but the bottoms better be black.

I felt a little pang about not being able to bring out the white belts and white purses too, and I don't even own any. But just knowing that I couldn't carry a white purse if I wanted to . . .

My black capri pants are my new uniform now. And that's okay, because when your mother's ancient Midwestern rules and regulations are happy, everybody's happy.

Eleven

The Journey of a Thousand Miles Is Sure to Be Littered with Tiny Bottles of Shampoo

Trip Planning Cent Un

'm so excited to begin Trip Planning Phase I for our trip to Paris and Rome later this year. I wish I were one of those people who can say, "Oh yes, we're going to Paris this summer." *Sigh*. And act like it's an everyday occurrence to get on an airplane and fly to a country where English as a Second Language is an actual second language or even a third or fourth.

I want to be the kind of person who, when in a conversation about something entirely unrelated to travel, will say, "We did that when we were in Paris last year. Or wait, was it last year's trip, or was it our fourth trip, in '06? I can't remember." *Hair flip*.

Or the person who will find the one not-so-wonderful thing about going to Paris and complain about it: "I hate getting sick in Paris. It's terrible and it can ruin your whole trip." *Gwyneth Paltrow pout*.

Who am I kidding? I don't want to be that person. I know that person and she's tiresome. If you're going to talk about your trip to Paris, it should be like this: "I'M SO EXCITED! I GET TO GO TO PARIS! OH MY GOD! YOU GUYS!"

And if I had a choice to go to Paris and get sick with a kidney stone and the accompanying vomiting, fever, and mind-bending pain, or not go at all and stay home pain-free, I'd take the stone and pass it by drinking the legal limit of wine.

Suffice it to say I will not be the least bit cool when I'm in Paris. I will be a virtual Clark Griswold. I'm a Hubbard girl, and going to Paris thrills the living shit out of me.

I say I get to start Trip Planning Phase I now, because we just bought our airline tickets today (followed by a short but spirited dance of joy), so there's no turning back. I've planned other trips down to what we were going to get on our Sbarro's pizza at the Atlanta airport, only to have the whole trip scrapped and my trip plans fizzle. So this time I waited until it was set in nonrefundable-ticket stone.

We've taken one other huge vacation as a family and that was four years ago, to Ireland and England. Because I had earned the reputation of over-planning to the nth degree, my family begged me to leave a few details to fate on that trip.

"But what if we can't find a restaurant in Kensington that can seat five in non-smoking at 7:15, within walking distance of the palace on June 3, Kensington Palace/Garden/Hyde Park/Upscale Shopping/Souvenir Day?"

They assured me it would all work out. So I agreed to lighten up and did not pre-plan one single meal for the entire trip. The result was that we actually couldn't find a restaurant in London when we were hungry one night, and ended up eating at the same Indian restaurant twice. We may as well have been at the hospital cafeteria waiting for a kidney stone to pass.

You can bet I won't let that happen again. I'm already looking up restaurants on the Internet and in the eleven travel guides I've borrowed and bought. I'm putting together days in which food and activities will seemingly fall out of the Parisian sky and land right in our laps. Don't be surprised if we whirl and turn and a dainty Nutella croissant is placed in our outstretched hands by a girl in a French maid costume. At dinner, we'll link arms and skip down one rue or another, and waiters will come dancing out with trays of escargot. My goal is to plan this trip so freaking thoroughly that we'll have no reason to return to either Paris or Rome ever.

I think I missed my calling as a travel agent.

That's Italian

Nine days in New York City will give you a new insight into the ethnic make-up of this country.

For example, if you live in the Midwest or Connecticut or Montana and you think there's a nationwide immigration problem and it's Mexicans sneaking across the border, stay in my hotel in Chinatown and tell me what you think of that after a couple of trips down East Broadway on a Tuesday afternoon. You will see hardly any Mexicans.

Because I was willing to ride the subways, I was able to crisscross the city and take in its multiple ethnicities within the space of a single day.

Multiply that by nine days and I can safely say that my favorite ethnic group, the Italians, came through with flying colors once again. Let me make the comparison between Chinatown and Little Italy, since they're right next to each other. Turning that corner from Canal Street onto Mulberry is like going from a busy Asian marketplace where salespeople are screaming at you to buy their bootleg DVDs, counterfeit handbags, raw fish, and jewelry to being transported to the flashback scene in *Godfather II*. You can actually hear a real accordion playing in a darkly lit bar that smells like pizzelles. Lord, give me strength. It's hard not to just go in and have an espresso.

The waiters stand out in front of the restaurants in Little Italy and seduce you right into a chair at one of their tables. A construction worker complimented me on my pedicure. A limo driver stopped and asked my sister and me if we were looking for somewhere to go have a drink. Okay, those last two things were kind of creepy, especially since my sisters and I are all on the wrong side of fifty, but you get the picture.

Occasionally there is some crossover. My sisters and I were having some of Vincent's famous spicy sauce, pasta, and wine, surrounded by black-and-white photos of Frank Sinatra and Paul Sorvino, when someone sneaked up behind me and said, "DVD? DVD?" I said no but she was back in a flash. "DVD? DVD?" She shoved a cover in front of my face.

"We're not buying anything," I snapped. For crying out loud, the four of us had already spent the equivalent of my Kiwanis Club college scholarship on pashminas in Chinatown. But right now I was almost melted into my chair—the wine, the sauce, the music, Paul Sorvino smiling down at me—do I *look* like I want to watch *Toy Story 3* right now?

The Chinatown merchants are clearly making more money. Remember when we were all afraid the Japanese were going to take over America because they were buying up all of our stock and their kids went to school year-round and kicked our asses in math? The new threat is the Chinese, and not because they own us but because we are handing out cold hard cash to them in exchange for things that will fall apart next week.

If we're making ethnic generalizations (and because I'm Irish, I'm allowed; we've got a dispensation from the pope), I would say that Chinese Americans are the hardest working, most entrepreneurial group in New York. Nobody's selling hotdogs on Broadway with as much zeal. The drug dealers in the Bronx aren't as enthusiastic. And uptown? Forget about it. Most of the shops on Madison Avenue are By Appointment Only.

The shops in Chinatown must be making as much in one hour as a single visit from a Kardashian to Versace. Their sales tactics, however obnoxious, are paying off, one I Heart New York T-shirt at a time. But I'll take an Italian waiter and whatever he's selling any day of the week.

Hotel Shampoo? Yes, Please

I'm having a hard time wrapping my head around the fact that I've had some great hair days on vacation. I would count my blessings, but I'm too busy trying to figure out what deal I inadvertently struck with the devil to have this prize land in my lap.

My experience has taught me that the vile combination of Not Wanting to Risk a Shampoo Explosion in Your Suitcase + Your Decision Not to Bring Your Own Tried-and-True Shampoo + Erroneous Thinking That a Nice Hotel Might Provide You with Some Decent Health and Beauty Aids + Holy Crap We're Paying How Much a Night at This Place? + More Naive, Stupid, Hopeful Thinking + Downward Spiral Upon Realization That Even the Waldorf-Fucking-Astoria Puts Dawn Dish Liquid in a Fancy Bottle and Calls It Shampoo + And I Really Want My Hair to Look Good in These Pictures Dammit = Unintentional Dreadlocks That Smell Like a Birthday Cake.

You would think for $200+ a night, we'd get a few squirts of Pureology so we wouldn't have to take a rat's nest into the hoity-toity piano bar at the end of the day. So imagine my surprise when my hair looked a little better than normal after the first two showers here.

"I don't know whether to use this stuff or steal it," I told my husband. I've never been tempted to not use the hotel shampoo so I could take more home to use in off-vacation days. But now I'm facing that dilemma.

I don't steal from hotels. Much. A year ago I accidentally took a really nice hanger from a bed and breakfast and was beside myself with regret.

"Should I mail it back to them?" I asked my husband.

"I'm sure they have more hangers in a guest closet somewhere," he said. "If you're the first person to take a hanger home, they haven't been in business long enough and it's time they joined the real world." A world of stealers, I guess. That's sad to me. I hoped they just wouldn't notice.

I do take the little bottles of shampoo and conditioner from hotels, because I understand that's permitted. I follow my old friend John's rule of authorized theft, which he taught me at Wendy's in Kent, Ohio. We were leaving when he walked over to the condiment station, opened the bottom cabinet, took a big pack of napkins, and walked out the door. When I asked him what he thought he was doing, he said, "You can't be accused of stealing something that is offered to you for free. Napkins are free at Wendy's, so I can take as many as I want." His house in Kent was full of oblong napkins, and his roommates may still not have run out of tiny ketchup, mustard, salt, and pepper packets.

I believe hotel shampoo, conditioner, soap, and hand lotion fall into that rule. But I don't take them for my personal use. With the intent of donating them to a women's shelter, I put them in big plastic bags, where they sit in my closet, crushed by tote bags and travel gear until they expire or turn into diamonds.

But now that I think of it, a homeless woman fleeing an abusive husband deserves better shampoo than that. If anyone should be indulged in a designer hair product, it's her. Imagine gathering up a few possessions and fleeing an asshole, making it safely to a shelter, where you share a bed with your own children and several other families, get a packet of supplies to go to the shower so you can make a good impression in court, and you see that the shampoo is from Days Inn. It could be the last straw for some women.

So for now, I'm going to just enjoy the use of this hotel shampoo, which I believe is the reason my hair looks better than average these days. We wrote down the ingredients, hoping to find something similar from Sally's. It has desert yucca in it. Also jojoba. It smells of expensive salon and not gas station bathroom air freshener. You'll know if I find it by my good hairdos.

Putting the Ass Back in First Class

Well, it finally happened. My husband, Mr. Silver Medallion frequent flyer, got upgraded to first class on a flight. He grabbed it—couldn't say yes fast enough—and left his wife and daughter in steerage.

Moo.

I rarely complain about air travel. I consider myself lucky enough to be flying in an aero-plane, something that used to be reserved for the rich and adventurous. People who complain about the inconvenience of air travel are in the same category as people who complain about the room service in Europe. If you're blessed enough to be there, complaining about it doesn't make you classy. We can see through that, you know.

So I really don't mind riding in coach with the rest of the mouth-breathing, fidgety, chatty populists. I don't mind being confined to a chair the same size as my daughter's American Girl doll's wheelchair. I don't complain if my tray table is crooked and there are bed bugs in my blanket. Leg room? If there's room for my foot, it's enough. Maybe I'm jealous, but I just don't see the advantage of riding in first class.

We once checked out the cost differences between flying first class and flying coach. It was going to be a long flight, and my husband was muttering something about deep vein thrombosis and how undignified it would be to die of a blood clot in international air space. The first class seat was thousands of dollars more than the coach seat. A quick check of Expedia says that a non-stop flight from West Palm Beach to New York in early December will run you $168. That same flight in first class is $928. A flight to Beijing will run you more than $15,000 in first class. What are they doing up there behind that curtain? Really, I want to know. With $15,000, you could buy a nice car. Or put a down payment on a house. Or you could stretch out your legs on one airplane ride and get a hot towel.

Given the choice, I'd curl up inside a dog crate with a couple of muscle re-laxers, tough it out, and take the difference in cash. I can think of about fifteen thousand things to spend that money on, and not just at the duty-free shop.

At least my husband didn't pay for his upgrade. Still, he took no small amount of glee in bragging about how he rode with the rich people while my daughter and I were back with the masses.

"So did you get a hot towel?" I asked him as sarcastically as I could.

"No," he answered. "But I got a backrub."

He better have been kidding.

Bassoons on a Plane

I was getting so excited about my upcoming trip to New York City in June, planning to eat some big sandwiches, do a lot of walking, take a bunch of pictures, and maybe visit with some old friends in New Jersey. But now every time I think about the trip I get a big knot in my stomach, because I can't figure out how to get my daughter's bassoon there.

It's too big to be a carry-on and it's too fragile to be a checked bag that the baggage handlers can play volleyball with.

I would just leave it at home except the whole reason for the trip is so that she can play her bassoon. She kind of needs it.

I would skip the flight and just drive there, except driving in Manhattan puts an even bigger knot in my stomach.

Shouldn't there be more transportation choices than driving a personal vehicle or flying in an airplane run by The Airlines, which seem to have a bug up their asses about our desire to take stuff with us when we go from Place A to Place B?

Thinking of all the professional musicians who make guest appearances in concerts all over the world, I thought there has to be a simple solution. When you see a bassoonist playing his bassoon, do you think, *well, he must be a local, because how else would he get the bassoon to where he needs to play?*

So I went onto some message boards and found a few bassoonists who had advice for traveling musicians. The advice boiled down to sneaking the bassoon onto the plane, even though it exceeds size limits and we live in a post-9/11 world.

Here are some actual quotes from the bullet points on one website:

"As the gate attendant takes your boarding pass, look him or her in the eye and smile, and say something friendly and polite if appropriate."

"Don't look down at your instrument."

"Hold the instrument in the hand farthest away, with your body casually blocking their view of it."

"As you head down the jetway or onto the tarmac, discreetly remove and pocket the gate-check tag, or, since it's usually attached to the case's handle, just make sure the tag is inside your hand."

"This is not a time to deliver a lecture about the instrument's value or fragility, or otherwise to suggest that you deserve special treatment."

"Don't make a stink."

This can't be right, I thought as I read these. None of the advice seemed to make any sense. It sounds like my daughter is supposed to feel guilty because she's flying to New York with a double reed instrument.

There's nothing dangerous about the bassoon, nothing beyond maybe a Terror Level Periwinkle. You could whack somebody silly with it, but there are better weapons. A Michener book would cause more pain. The thing about the bassoon is it's large. It breaks down into smaller tubes, but when packed correctly in a regulation case, it's still pretty large and heavy as all get-out.

The bassoon is actually the smallest of the three instruments my daughter plays. Last summer, when she played the cello, we had to rearrange the furniture in the living room to find a spot for it. She also plays the piano. I guess I should be grateful we aren't traveling with either of those two instruments. But now I know why piccolo and flute players have that smug little grin on their faces all the time. You could smuggle a piccolo in a body cavity if you had to.

Finding little solace on Web message boards, I looked for a Musical Instruments and Other Fragile Items clause in the airline website. There is one and this is what it says:

> If the musical instrument is large and you'd like to carry it on, you may need to purchase a seat for the instrument, provided there is availability. The instrument or equipment must be secured in a window seat and cannot be secured in the first row or emergency exit rows.

If we buy the bassoon a seat and it gets the window, I want its pretzel snack and instant coffee. Does it get its own carry-on bag and under-the-seat luggage for reeds? Will it want to share my crossword puzzle for the trip? Does it know any good word games? As fun as it sounds—especially the possibility of dressing it up—I decided it would be expensive and silly to buy a plane ticket for a bassoon.

I decided to go straight to the top: a customer service phone-answerer at the airline.

"I wouldn't worry about it," she said. She took down the dimensions of the bassoon case and said, "Yeah, it is too large for a carry-on, but it'll fit. You should be fine." She did not see the seriousness of having to last-minute check a flimsy, unlocked case containing a multi-thousand-dollar musical instrument and my daughter's future. She also did not agree to my suggestion that she put *You should be fine* in writing.

I was so looking forward to waving a piece of paper around at airport security. I think that's "making a stink."

Flying Turns Me into a Second Grader

A recent trip required that I fly in an airplane, which means that for 2.75 hours, I was back to being in elementary school.

Flying on an airplane turns everyone into a second grader. I'm not ancient and I'm not terribly sophisticated, but even I'm embarrassed at the way I sit there in my seat, slightly hunched over, looking up with hopeful puppy eyes at the flight attendant, waiting to see what she's bringing me.

Snack? Is it snack time yet? Oh, just the drinks? What should I get, what should I get? Last time I got apple juice, and I got all excited and drank it too fast and got a stomachache.

You don't dare go back to your magazine, because as slow as she's making her way down that aisle, if you take your eyes off her, she'll go right past you. And you can forget about getting your juice. That cart doesn't have reverse.

I don't want to point any fingers, but I think the airlines do this on purpose. They know we're getting a deal on those tickets. When you can fly across the sky in a big metal object both ways for the price of a nice dinner out for four people, you know you'll have to pay a price for that. And the price is to be a humiliated seven-year-old while you're in the thing.

Take the seats: They're narrow enough that you're forced to sit with your hands on your lap. The seat backs are curved so that you're slightly hunched. If you were a dog or a concubine you would be in a forced submissive position. But you're on an airplane, so you're in a forced second-grade submissive position.

You're unable to do anything with your legs that makes them look the least bit attractive, no matter how short your skirt or how sleek your pants. You're unable to straighten your back enough to make your boobs even appear to the naked eye. You have to keep both feet flat on the floor, your hands on your lap, and your head slightly bowed so that when you make eye contact with the ~~headmaster~~ flight attendant, you're looking up in a pathetic way. What a crossed leg and a hand on a hip wouldn't do for my self-esteem on an airplane. I might have enough confidence to hail my own cab from the airport to the hotel.

As the flight attendant gets closer with—what? What is it? I THINK IT'S SNACKS THIS TIME!—you anxiously put your tray table down and get ready.

The snack is coming, the snack is coming, the snack is coming . . . Don't you dare take your eyes off her.

One time I said, "No thank you, nothing for me," and the flight attendant cocked her head and said, "Are you sure?" I had been sure, very sure, but suddenly I doubted my second-grade decision-making skills and had a small pitter-patter panic. Great. Now I have to decide which snack I want while she's standing right here by my seat, staring at me and tapping her foot. My eyes darted to the cart's selections and I quickly blurted out, "Popcorn chips!" Then I got them and saw they were caramel flavored. Caramel flavored! Shit! I hate goddamn caramel-flavored popcorn chips! I ate them obediently and without a fuss.

And snacks on the airplane have changed. You bet your ass they've changed. No more peanuts, because someone was allergic. You watch, we'll be down to apples and granola bars by 2018, because someone's mom called the main office.

International flights are even worse. The "meal" they give you isn't fit for a feral cat, but it's four courses that you eat with a plastic fork with zero elbow room. You're unwrapping pungent chicken in an even pungenter gravy, and buttering your little roll with T-Rex arms, feeding yourself like a squirrel. And you eat every bite with the eagerness of a maximum-security prisoner.

The first time I flew across the Atlantic I was surprised to learn about the mandatory naptime.

"Please turn out your light. Passengers are sleeping," the flight attendant said to me, just as I was settling in with a book. On the ground in any first- or second-world nation, I would have reminded that little bitch that I was an adult and could stay up all night reading if I wanted to, that my book was rated R and had lots of swear words and sex in it, and that she is not the boss of me. But in the air, I meekly closed my book, turned off my light, and took my scheduled nap.

My only consolation is that everyone else on the plane is in the second grade too. In the unlikely scenario that Hillary Clinton was flying coach, she would be the nerdy goody-two-shoes who was sucking up to the flight attendant by paying close attention to the safety instructions.

Airplanes have the regular cast of characters from the second grade. There are bullies, show-offs, cranky-pantses, and wallflowers. Even kids who will try to sneak out their toys after we've plainly been told that all toys have to be shut off.

He's not following the rules! I've whispered to myself as I sat with my crumpled-up baby napkin in my fist, waiting for the flight attendant to make her way down the aisle to take our trash.

And if someone throws up everyone will remember it forever.

Twelve

A Ghost Writer Doesn't Write About Ghosts and Other Things You Should Know About Writers

Introducing Guest Blogger: Me

My sister Pam was supposed to guest-write my blog on Saturday. But we went to Miami Beach and had too many mojitos to organize thoughts or anything else, so we postponed it until Sunday. She sat down to write it after I promised to set her up with a bonus glass of wine late-delivered right to her keyboard. She wrote a few paragraphs, deleted them, wrote a few more, deleted them, and said, "I can't do this." The rest of us were watching the Oscars and talking, and hardly noticed she was even at the computer.

She of course could *so* do this. If it was a matter of not enough wine, I could have accommodated her. We've been making daily runs to Winn Dixie during this sisters' get-together to buy reinforcements. Winn Dixie has been showing her appreciation by putting all the Kendall Jackson on sale all week.

Truth be told, I was happy to sit down at the computer at 12:30 a.m. Monday and write a short blog post. My sisters are multitalented women to be reckoned with. Even my mother-in-law said, "I'm sick of hearing about how creative your sisters are." Among the fun we're having this week: We've been to a quilt shop and bought supplies to make a couple different things; we're making the envelope liners for my niece's wedding invitations; they took pictures of designer clothes, bedding, and linens in upscale shops so they can go home to their basement sewing rooms and make them for a fraction of the cost; and they bought Italian writing paper to make stuff out of.

It's like shopping with Coco Chanel. I tag along like the sister that was switched at birth. Somewhere in a double-wide trailer, there's a family saying, "What's with little Miss Thang here, color contrast-coordinating the curtains with the placemats?"

So if I'm the only one willing to pour another glass of wine and write a blog at—what is it now?—12:45 a.m., it makes me feel pretty good about myself. And a sisters' get-together is all about self-esteem. If you end it with less than you started with, you're not doing it right.

Pam said she wanted to write about our brother, who gets left out of a lot of these things because he's a boy. But we love him, and we probably should get the word out on that via the Internet. Then she said maybe she'd write about how women are so much better at bonding than men, knowing that some of our husbands have tried this sort of thing before with less success. Then she was going to write about our childhoods and growing up in a working-class neighborhood.

"Oh, cripes, keep it light," someone deadpanned. We're not dramatic or sentimental, and somebody who's having trouble writing a blog isn't going to get a lot of sympathy out of this crowd.

She kept it so light her page was blank when she grabbed her wineglass and sat down to watch Jeff Bridges accept his Oscar.

If You Don't Have Anything Nice to Say, You're Not Alone

When I first started writing on the Wonderful World Wide Web (that's what we called it way back then; it was a happier, less cynical time), I got all excited when I found out that our articles would be open to comments from readers. I may as well have been wearing a camo diaper, I was such a babe in the woods. I actually thought I would be engaged in a lively, spirited exchange on issues, with suggestions and personal stories that would lead to a better understanding and possibly more follow-up stories.

Instead, what I got was this:

Yu suck
This is terible
You don't know anything. This was not what I was looking for.
You people are a bunch of morons. If you don't like staying at home with
your kids, get a job. How hard is that.
看看我的網站, 我希望你會喜歡你所看到的

Supposing that the last one wasn't some ancient Chinese curse, this is a pretty good sample of what I get in a typical week. For every four nasty-grams, I get one—well, maybe not-so-nasty-gram. Luckily, I can control whether to preview the comments and allow or disallow. I do a lot of disallowing.

I'm certainly not alone. There's enough hate out there to go around to every single person who shows up on the Internet. At the bar of life, the haters can say "Set 'em up, Joe! The next one's on me!" because lashings are cheap and easy. You don't even have to know how to spell or talk good and stuff.

Karen Sandstrom wrote a guest column in *The Plain Dealer* about the pain of sending her firstborn child to college in Colorado. She was dealing with it by eating Peppermint Patties and other guilty pleasures. Really a sweet column. Innocuous enough? Think again. Within an hour, comments like this started showing up:

The daughter was (sic) probably couldn't get away from this woman fast enough. Hundreds of thousands of students go away to college every year. People are sending their families and loved ones off to war and dangerous deployments. where the Amerian (sic) flag on their uniform is a bulls eye (sic) in the cross-hairs of a crazed militant insurgent. Seriously? And you worry about sending your kid off to a cushy safe college nestled in the Rocky Mountains? Get a life lady bury your head in a gallon of Ice cream. You need a reality check.

Another reader seemed to disagree about the safe part:

> *Luckily, your daughter is statistically more likely to flunk, develop a drug problem and put her tuition up her nose, or get knocked-up and leave college before she finishes. So she may be home with a pint of Haagen Daas (sic) before you know it. At just over $21,000 per semester for an out of state student living on campus, it's fairly likely that her debt load at graduation will bring her back home to live for a decade or so. Buy a cat.*

Do these people know how to party or what? Let's talk about campus rape too! And meningitis, low job placement, late-teen suicide, the fact that many mental illnesses strike at around age twenty. Oh, right, and the possibility that we'll all be dead from a nuclear bomb within four years anyway. That poor girl will be going to community college in no time, and the mom will be rethinking her writing career.

I don't know who the people are who nasty up my Internet party every day, but I'm glad I don't know any of them in my real life. I know they live all over the country, but in which neighborhoods exactly? I'd like the addresses so I can continue to avoid them like registered sex offenders.

When I was featured in *The Wall Street Journal*, some nasty comments were tacked onto the end of the story. I stopped reading them when someone criticized my kitchen decor. Call me fat and ugly, say I'm a loser, question my intelligence, whatever. But keep your negative vibe off my granite countertops.

That's why I was so glad to hear that Tina Fey had struck back. When she accepted her Golden Globe award for *30 Rock*, she said, "If you ever start to feel too good about yourself they have this thing called the Internet and, um, you can find a lot of people there who don't like you." And then she told those people to suck it.

Let's join her. Hey, Internet haters: Suck it. But I mean that in the nicest way.

Edwin Newman, We Hardly Knew You, You're, Your

I was so sorry to hear that Edwin Newman died. My copy of *Strictly Speaking* was possibly the first responsible book I read without it being assigned to me.

I bought it because I wanted it and I read it because I wanted to. I was twenty and probably more mature than I am now. Definitely more serious than I am now.

Journalism school threatened to ruin me as a personable, likable human being. In college, despite the fact that my roommates were mostly fashion models, PE majors, a cage dancer, and "college students" in quotes only, I spent an inordinate amount of time with fellow writers. The result was that I thought the whole world knew the difference between *their, there,* and *they're* and that they cared.

Like all bubbles, it was an unhealthy atmosphere. I was editing my junk mail. I was criticizing people who didn't know who their congressman was. I was a drag. For fun, my boyfriend and I would go to lectures. We once participated in an audience performance of Handel's *The Messiah*. But enough about me and my nerdly ways.

Edwin Newman. I pored over *Strictly Speaking* and absorbed all the rules and nitpicky criticisms of a language that is misused and abused.

Then I graduated college and got a real job in the adult world, where my writer friends and I were even more of a minority, and the world was seemingly overrun with fashion models, aerobics instructors, cage dancers, and people whose job descriptions were in quotation marks.

And they were all spelling things incorrectly and misusing the language somethin' turrible.

So in a moment weakened by three beers at the Backstage Lounge, I started a club with my husband and our friend George. The club was called The King's English and we, as members, planned to work for the improvement of the English language, mostly by writing to businesses about their signs. We had gotten fed up with the Kozy Korner and the Kountry Kitchen and other misspellings for the sake of being cute.

The club didn't last long. We may have gotten to the fourth beer, but I'm not even sure about that. We tried to recruit a new member, Larry Quinn, who was a copyeditor where we worked, and he just kept shaking his head and saying, "No, no, no . . . you can't do that. That won't work. Aw, geez . . ."

Larry felt as strongly about preserving the language as we did, but he thought we were just being stupid.

He was right. We started to write down some parameters of what was right and what was wrong, and when we got to businesses that overused Olde and Shoppe, we couldn't decide whether that was bad/corny/sickening/wrong or just going back to the original English . . . like the King's English. So you see the problem.

I still think Edwin Newman would have been happy to see that we at least tried. Since then, I've dangled a lot of participles and mismatched my subjects and verbs. I make mistakes in my writing and can always—always—find an error if I just keep reading my pieces enough times.

Hopefully, no one has noticed. And if you got that, you can join my club.

A Writer's Nerdist Colony

I spent the past four days at a writers' conference, and I feel like I just left church camp with a bunch of friendship bracelets.

Anytime you get a group of people who do the same thing for a living or pursue the same hobby and you stick them in the same hotel conference room wing at the same time, you're looking at a nerd-fest.

Whether it's a Girl Scout camp, a quilters' conference, a weekly newspaper editors' retreat, or a Renaissance Faire—and I am here to proudly say that I've been to all of these—something happens to the air when you get too much similar obsession in the same vicinity. We all turn into geeks.

This writers' conference had all the elements. There were writers from all over the US and some foreign countries. There were poets in dreadlocks and loose weaves. There were crime writers in beards, little round glasses, and hats. There was a guy in a kilt and all the accoutrements except the bagpipes. There were twenty-five-year-old cookbook writers. There were lawyers with briefcases who write utopian fiction. There were housewives from Colorado who write paranormal romance. Did you know that Steampunk is a genre? I do. Now.

Despite all our differences, because we all put words down on paper, that one commonality triggered the nerd vibe big-time. I knew there were writers at the conference who wanted to think we were reminiscent of Paris in the 1920s, when Ernest Hemingway, F. Scott Fitzgerald, and Gertrude Stein drank a lot of whiskey and philosophized all night long. Yeah. No. Not that. We were more like Comic Con.

I learned a lot at the conference, about what book I want to write next, how to market my first book, how to outline, what I can write off on my taxes, how to handle rejection without getting snot all over my laptop, and that some book publishers are a little bit arrogant on their best day and some book publishers are as nice as my nicest brother-in-law on their worst day.

But what I learned the most was that people in their sixties and seventies are rocking the world right now.

I don't know what that age group is doing at other festivals, but the ones at the writers' conferences are kicking ass. I saw a lot of people a lot older than me attending workshops on "Social Meetia: Building Your Web Presence," which is about building your platform; "Blog Your Way to a Book Deal," which is about building your platform; "Discoverability in the Age of Social Media," which is about building your platform; and "Building Your Platform."

And they were taking notes. On their iPad minis.

Not a single person over sixty said, "I don't tweet on The Facebook, so can you tell me what color pen to use when I send out press releases to New York City?" These people are not only embracing the fast-changing world of book publishing, they are giving it a bear hug and then French kissing it and humping it in the alley behind the hotel.

"I'm going to ask a stupid question," one woman said in the Q&A after one session. *Oh boy. Here we go*, I thought. And then she asked a question that was so intelligent even the presenter couldn't answer without Googling it under the podium.

I brag a lot about my mother-in-law. I love to tell stories about how she uses Twitter and Instagram to keep up with her children, grandchildren, and great-grandchildren. We love to tell her story to people in their late fifties to shame them into not saying things like "I don't get this new technology." My mother-in-law has become a poster child for what senior citizens can become, simply by being willing to adapt.

After this conference, I realize that her job is done. She can just drop that mic. Her demographic has caught up with her—the writer subcategory anyway—and they are carrying the football all the way to the end zone.

And that's a mixed metaphor, which I learned at "Using Mixed Metaphors in Your YA Fiction," is about building your platform.

Now I Will Admit to a Bunch of Stupid Stuff

I'm closing out the books on my little at-home writing business for this year, and I can now honestly say that I make a living by being a doofus.

I'm the kind of writer who gets paid to admit that she once accidentally gave her toddler a margarita (calm down, perfect parents; did I not just say accidentally? It doesn't count if it's more neglect than abuse), that I got my first manicure at thirty-five, my first massage at fifty-four, and I still know all the words to the Lawson's commercial. I sing it out loud when I'm home alone. I also remember—and when I'm alone perform—the first part of my Doris Furney dance routine to *The March of the Siamese Children*. This is about as liberating as it sounds.

Unlike people who make their living being beautiful or sophisticated or smart or a decent parent, building a business around being someone who makes mistakes is, frankly, awesome. It's like always being around childhood friends who know you too well, making it impossible to put on airs and pretend you're something you're not.

1. You don't have to worry about tripping, falling awkwardly, and having people think badly of you. That's your job.
2. Any self-improvement notions like learning a hip foreign language or eating kale and other trendy foods that make you seem savvy? You can say forget that and watch another episode of *Hoarders* and finish the Cheez-Its.

Your persona is all about TV binge watching, not knowing any state capitals and mispronouncing French words. In fact, your career depends on it. It's very, very hard to make a fool out of someone like that.

If you've read my blog you already know about the sippy-cup margaritas and all the singing. I thought the new year would be a good time to get a few more revelations off my chest.

- I get Yosemite and Yellowstone mixed up. I didn't know one was in California until last year. In fact, I still don't know where either is on the map, and I don't expect to ever learn and remember any of it.
- I mispronounced merlot once and my neighbor Brian never let me forget it.
- I took a memory test recently to raise awareness for Alzheimer's and got a 17 percent. That score put me in the category of *You are not only prone to get Alzheimer's, you probably already have it, and if not, getting it will not be a problem because you have no brain synapses left to misfire.*
- I love math but if I think too much about infinity I have a panic attack and start to sweat.
- I thought hyperventilating was that thing that happens when you hold in tears in second grade and you inhale in little uncontrollable gasps. It wasn't until I was in labor with my first baby and numbness had moved up from my hands to my elbow region that a nurse told me what a dumbass I was. I made a good case for why that second grade breathing thing should be called *hyperventilating*, and what we now know as hyperventilating should be called *that numby hands thing*, but no one could hear me through the paper bag.
- I allowed myself to be videotaped performing the Lollipop Guild song, knowing it would be put on YouTube. I can never run for president now.
- I say "thank you" when I give money to street beggars. I've decided it's easier to think of something they're doing for me and the world than to try to break myself of the habit.

All of this and a number of things I haven't told you about yet make up my career. When people ask me what I do, it goes something like this:

"Oooh, you're a writer? Really? What do you write?"

"Well, um, yeah, good question; I—"

"Do you write romance? Are you like Danielle Steel? Do you write like *Fifty Shades of Grey? The Hunger Games?* Are you like a mystery writer? Do you write about dogs? You should write about dogs. I read *The Notebook* and it changed my life. Do you write stuff like *The Notebook?*"

"No, I pretty much write down stories about stupid stuff I did and then sometimes people laugh and then sometimes I get some money for it. So, I do that."

"You should try writing something like *The Notebook.*"

Acknowledgments

To my family—Tim, Mike, Alex, Jack, and Caroline—thank you for giving me so much to write about. You are the funniest and best all-round human beings I know.

To my siblings and in-laws, cousins first and second and various times removed, thank you for being proud of me when it seemed like I wasn't doing much good at all.

A big thank-you to my friends who read my stuff when I know for a fact they have more important things to do.

To my teachers, from kindergarten through the adult education class I took three years ago, thank you for devoting your life to teaching people like me how to be smart. Also how to do algebra, because I *did so* use that after high school.

Thanks to all of my faithful readers and fellow bloggers whose paths crossed mine, some with whom I became real-life friends. My friend Skippy will live in my heart forever.

Thank you to Angie Kiesling, my editor for this book, as well as everyone else who gently and politely alerts me of errors in my writing.

About the Author

Diane Laney Fitzpatrick writes the humor blog *Just Humor Me* and is the author of *Home Sweet Homes: How Bundt Cakes, Bubble Wrap, and My Accent Helped Me Survive Nine Moves.* She lives in San Francisco. You can find her online at DianeLaneyFitzpatrick.com.

www.ingramcontent.com/pod-product-compliance
Lightning Source LLC
Chambersburg PA
CBHW060927040426
42445CB00011B/825